Hernando de Soto

and the Explorers of the American South

General Editor

William H. Goetzmann
Jack S. Blanton, Sr., Chair in History
  University of Texas at Austin

Consulting Editor

Tom D. Crouch
Chairman, Department of Aeronautics
  National Air and Space Museum
  Smithsonian Institution

WORLD EXPLORERS

Introductory Essay by Michael Collins

CHELSEA HOUSE PUBLISHERS

New York · Philadelphia

On the cover Sixteenth-century Spanish map of the New World; portrait of de Soto.

Chelsea House Publishers
Editor-in-Chief Remmel Nunn
Managing Editor Karyn Gullen Browne
Copy Chief Juliann Barbato
Picture Editor Adrian G. Allen
Art Director Maria Epes
Deputy Copy Chief Mark Rifkin
Assistant Art Director Noreen Romano
Series Design Loraine Machlin
Manufacturing Manager Gerald Levine
Systems Manager Lindsey Ottman
Production Manager Joseph Romano
Production Coordinator Marie Claire Cebrián

World Explorers
Senior Editor Sean Dolan

Staff for HERNANDO DE SOTO AND THE EXPLORERS
OF THE AMERICAN SOUTH
Copy Editor Joseph Roman
Editorial Assistant Martin Mooney
Picture Researcher Nisa Rauschenberg
Senior Designer Basia Niemczyc

3 5 7 9 8 6 4 2

Library of Congress Cataloging-in-Publication Data

Whitman, Sylvia.
Hernando de Soto and the explorers of the American South/Sylvia Whitman.
p.   cm.—(World explorers)
Includes bibliographical references and index.
Summary: An account of the exploration of the American South by Hernando de Soto, Ponce de León, and others.
ISBN 0-7910-1301-4
      0-7910-1524-6 (pbk.)
1. Soto, Hernando de, ca. 1500–1542—Juvenile literature.
2. Southern States—Discovery and exploration—Juvenile literature.
3. Explorers—American—Biography—Juvenile literature.
4. Explorers—Spain—Biography—Juvenile literature.
5. Spaniards—Southern States—History—16th century—Juvenile literature. [1. Southern States—Discovery and exploration.
2. Explorers.] I. Title. II. Series.
E125.S7W47   90-15569
970.01'6'092—dc20   CIP
[B]   AC

CONTENTS

Into the Unknown...7
Michael Collins

The Reader's Journey...9
William H. Goetzmann

ONE   Conquistadores and Indians 13

TWO   First Contacts..25

THREE   The Conquest Mentality 47

    Photo Essay: The Shock of the New.........................57

FOUR   No Turning Back......................................69

FIVE   The Death of a Dream 81

SIX   The Empty-Handed Return 95

    Further Reading 106

    Chronology 108

    Index...110

WORLD EXPLORERS

THE EARLY EXPLORERS

Herodotus and the Explorers of the Classical Age
Marco Polo and the Medieval Explorers
The Viking Explorers

THE FIRST GREAT AGE OF DISCOVERY

Jacques Cartier, Samuel de Champlain, and the Explorers of Canada
Christopher Columbus and the First Voyages to the New World
From Coronado to Escalante: The Explorers of the Spanish Southwest
Hernando de Soto and the Explorers of the American South
Sir Francis Drake and the Struggle for an Ocean Empire
Vasco da Gama and the Portuguese Explorers
La Salle and the Explorers of the Mississippi
Ferdinand Magellan and the Discovery of the World Ocean
Pizarro, Orellana, and the Exploration of the Amazon
The Search for the Northwest Passage
Giovanni da Verrazano and the Explorers of the Atlantic Coast

THE SECOND GREAT AGE OF DISCOVERY

Roald Amundsen and the Quest for the South Pole
Daniel Boone and the Opening of the Ohio Country
Captain James Cook and the Explorers of the Pacific
The Explorers of Alaska
John Charles Frémont and the Great Western Reconnaissance
Alexander von Humboldt, Colossus of Exploration
Lewis and Clark and the Route to the Pacific
Alexander Mackenzie and the Explorers of Canada
Robert Peary and the Quest for the North Pole
Zebulon Pike and the Explorers of the American Southwest
John Wesley Powell and the Great Surveys of the American West
Jedediah Smith and the Mountain Men of the American West
Henry Stanley and the European Explorers of Africa
Lt. Charles Wilkes and the Great U.S. Exploring Expedition

THE THIRD GREAT AGE OF DISCOVERY

Apollo to the Moon
The Explorers of the Undersea World
The First Men in Space
The Mission to Mars and Beyond
Probing Deep Space

CHELSEA HOUSE PUBLISHERS

Into the Unknown

Michael Collins

It is difficult to define most eras in history with any precision, but not so the space age. On October 4, 1957, it burst on us with little warning when the Soviet Union launched *Sputnik*, a 184-pound cannonball that circled the globe once every 96 minutes. Less than 4 years later, the Soviets followed this first primitive satellite with the flight of Yury Gagarin, a 27-year-old fighter pilot who became the first human to orbit the earth. The Soviet Union's success prompted President John F. Kennedy to decide that the United States should "land a man on the moon and return him safely to earth" before the end of the 1960s. We now had not only a space age but a space race.

I was born in 1930, exactly the right time to allow me to participate in Project Apollo, as the U.S. lunar program came to be known. As a young man growing up, I often found myself too young to do the things I wanted—or suddenly too old, as if someone had turned a switch at midnight. But for Apollo, 1930 was the perfect year to be born, and I was very lucky. In 1966 I enjoyed circling the earth for three days, and in 1969 I flew to the moon and laughed at the sight of the tiny earth, which I could cover with my thumbnail.

How the early explorers would have loved the view from space! With one glance Christopher Columbus could have plotted his course and reassured his crew that the world was indeed round. In 90 minutes Magellan could have looked down at every port of call in the *Victoria's* three-year circumnavigation of the globe. Given a chance to map their route from orbit, Lewis and Clark could have told President Jefferson that there was no easy Northwest Passage but that a continent of exquisite diversity awaited their scrutiny.

In a physical sense, we have already gone to most places that we can. That is not to say that there are not new adventures awaiting us deep in the sea or on the red plains of Mars, but more important than reaching new places will be understanding those we have already visited. There are vital gaps in our understanding of how our planet works as an ecosystem and how our planet fits into the infinite order of the universe. The next great age may well be the age of assimilation, in which we use microscope and telescope to evaluate what we have discovered and put that knowledge to use. The adventure of being first to reach may be replaced by the satisfaction of being first to grasp. Surely that is a form of exploration as vital to our well-being, and perhaps even survival, as the distinction of being the first to explore a specific geographical area.

The explorers whose stories are told in the books of this series did not just sail perilous seas, scale rugged mountains, traverse blistering deserts, dive to the depths of the ocean, or land on the moon. Their voyages and expeditions were journeys of mind as much as of time and distance, through which they—and all of mankind—were able to reach a greater understanding of our universe. That challenge remains, for all of us. The imperative is to see, to understand, to develop knowledge that others can use, to help nurture this planet that sustains us all. Perhaps being born in 1975 will be as lucky for a new generation of explorer as being born in 1930 was for Neil Armstrong, Buzz Aldrin, and Mike Collins.

The Reader's Journey

William H. Goetzmann

This volume is one of a series that takes us with the great explorers of the ages on bold journeys over the oceans and the continents and into outer space. As we travel along with these imaginative and courageous journeyers, we share their adventures and their knowledge. We also get a glimpse of that mysterious and inextinguishable fire that burned in the breast of men such as Magellan and Columbus—the fire that has propelled all those throughout the ages who have been driven to leave behind family and friends for a voyage into the unknown.

No one has ever satisfactorily explained the urge to explore, the drive to go to the "back of beyond." It is certain that it has been present in man almost since he began walking erect and first ventured across the African savannas. Sparks from that same fire fueled the transoceanic explorers of the Ice Age, who led their people across the vast plain that formed a land bridge between Asia and North America, and the astronauts and scientists who determined that man must reach the moon.

Besides an element of adventure, all exploration involves an element of mystery. We must not confuse exploration with discovery. Exploration is a purposeful human activity—a search for something. Discovery may be the end result of that search; it may also be an accident, as when Columbus found a whole new world while search-ing for the Indies. Often, the explorer may not even realize the full significance of what he has discovered, as was the case with Columbus. Exploration, on the other hand, is the product of a cultural or individual curiosity; it is a unique process that has enabled mankind to know and understand the world's oceans, continents, and polar re-gions. It is at the heart of scientific thinking. One of its most significant aspects is that it teaches people to ask the right questions; by doing so, it forces us to reevaluate what we think we know and understand. Thus knowledge pro-gresses, and we are driven constantly to a new awareness and appreciation of the universe in all its infinite variety.

The motivation for exploration is not always pure. In his fascination with the new, man often forgets that others have been there before him. For example, the popular notion of the discovery of America overlooks the complex Indian civilizations that had existed there for thousands of years before the arrival of Europeans. Man's desire for conquest, riches, and fame is often linked inextricably with his quest for the unknown, but a story that touches so closely on the human essence must of necessity treat war as well as peace, avarice with generosity, both pride and humility, frailty and greatness. The story of exploration is above all a story of humanity and of man's understanding of his place in the universe.

The WORLD EXPLORERS series has been divided into four sections. The first treats the explorers of the ancient world, the Viking explorers of the 9th through the 11th centuries, and Marco Polo and the medieval explorers. The rest of the series is divided into three great ages of exploration. The first is the era of Columbus and Magellan: the period spanning the 15th and 16th centuries, which saw the dis-covery and exploration of the New World and the world ocean. The second might be called the age of science and imperialism, the era made possible by the scientific ad-vances of the 17th century, which witnessed the discovery of the world's last two undiscovered continents, Australia and Antarctica, the mapping of all the continents and oceans, and the establishment of colonies all over the world. The third great age refers to the most ambitious quests of the 20th century—the probing of space and of the ocean's depths.

As we reach out into the darkness of outer space and other galaxies, we come to better understand how our ancestors confronted *oecumene*, or the vast earthly unknown. We learn once again the meaning of an unknown 18th-century sea captain's advice to navigators:

> And if by chance you make a landfall on the shores of another sea in a far country inhabited by savages and barbarians, remember you this: the greatest danger and the surest hope lies not with fires and arrows but in the quicksilver hearts of men.

At its core, exploration is a series of moral dramas. But it is these dramas, involving new lands, new people, and exotic ecosystems of staggering beauty, that make the explorers' stories not only moral tales but also some of the greatest adventure stories ever recorded. They represent the process of learning in its most expansive and vivid forms. We see that real life, past and present, transcends even the adventures of the starship *Enterprise*.

Conquistadores and Indians

On September 15, 1539, the conquistador Hernando de Soto and his small, weary army of Spaniards welcomed the sight of Napituca, a pleasant Timucuan Indian village in north central Florida about 20 miles southeast of the present-day town of Live Oak. In little more than 3 months, de Soto's expedition had trekked over 200 miles through the uncharted wilderness, slogging through swamps, scavenging for cabbage and watercress, sweltering under the tropical sun. Because of the frequent barrages of arrows from hostile Indians, the men dared not remove their heavy armor, and they even wore padded cotton jackets underneath it as extra protection and covered their horses with blankets.

Hunger was also a constant worry. For a party of about 500 Europeans and an unknown number of Indian captives, food was always in short supply. In many villages, the marchers found maize but no one to prepare it, since the native inhabitants usually fled to avoid being pressed into service as cooks and porters. Often too tired (or unwilling; such tasks were considered to be worthy only of servants) to beat grain on logs, sift flour through their shirts of mail, or bake bread over a fire, the hungry explorers usually subsisted on raw corn. At least in Napituca, the chief, Vitachuco, had ordered a feast.

But the conquistadores could not relax for long. Indian captives informed Juan Ortiz, the expedition's translator, that Vitachuco had cooperated with the explorers under

Vitachuco, the chief at the Timucuan village of Napituca, greets Hernando de Soto and his men. The chief planned to trick the conquistadores by offering them a feast and then launching a surprise attack, but word of his scheme reached de Soto, who readied his lancers, pikers, and swordsmen for battle.

De Soto gained power and prestige as a captain for Francisco Pizarro during the conquest of the Incas in Peru. He used this experience to secure the position of adelantado, or colonial governor, of Florida.

duress and was planning a surprise attack. Once apprised of this, de Soto and his captains secretly readied their lancers, pikers, swordsmen, halberdiers, and harquebusiers for battle.

According to one account, Vitachuco invited de Soto to review his warriors on a plain outside the village, where the Indians had hidden their bows and arrows in the grass. Playing along, the Spanish leader accepted with pleasure but insisted that his soldiers line up with him for a mock battle. Each ready to deceive the other, the two commanders strolled onto the field together. Suddenly, de Soto signaled for a trumpet to be sounded, leaped upon a dapple-gray horse named Aceytuno, and led the charge.

Such boldness—some would say foolhardiness—was typical of the 39-year-old governor of Cuba and *adelantado* (colonial governor) of Florida. In the early decades of the 16th century, several shipwrecked sailors and ill-fated adventurers had reconnoitered the coast of the Florida Peninsula, but no one had penetrated the interior of the North American mainland, a vast territory that the Spaniards hoped would yield precious metals to rival the riches of Mexico and Peru. Even before the great silver strikes in Mexico in the 1540s, wealth from New Spain had helped King Charles (Charles I of Spain, Charles V of the Holy Roman Empire) finance his wars of expansion with the royal share—a fifth of all the booty. When de Soto, a hero of the conquest of Central and South America, applied for a governorship in the New World, it cost the king nothing to grant him a string of titles and concessions. If the adelantado did unearth gold, both he and his ruler would benefit. At the very least, the expedition would strengthen Spain's claim to Florida, in which its rivals England and France were showing an interest.

Such a risky venture appealed to a restless veteran such as de Soto. In Peru, de Soto had profited as a captain under Francisco Pizarro, the ruthless Spanish conqueror of the powerful Inca Empire, but in Florida he would command, earning both *escudos* (gold coins) and glory. Graceful, with a dark but merry face, de Soto excelled in horsemanship, competent in both the old straight-seated saddle of the knights of the Middle Ages and the new, light Moorish saddle (*a la genita*) with short stirrups. As a professional soldier, he did not tolerate weakness; some of his contemporaries called him rash, cruel, and stubborn. He expected loyalty and obedience, but no more than he gave to the Crown and to the church. De Soto inspired his men by example, through his willingness to share every hardship with them, both in battle and on the march.

Just as they differ in their assessment of the governor, the four different contemporary accounts of the expedition do not concur on the exact circumstances, date, location, or troop count of the fray at Napituca. The background of each author colors his chronicle. The factor Luis Hernandez de Biedma traces the wanderings of the explorers in a cool and lean style befitting a financier. Admiration for the panache of the adelantado tempered by disgust over his unjust treatment of Native Americans shapes the published narratives of a Gentleman of Elvas, an unidentified Portuguese noble. In his diary, Rodrigo Ranjel, de Soto's secretary, also documents the ruthlessness of his boss. The Inca, Garcilaso de la Vega, was the only one of the four chroniclers who was not an eyewitness to the events he describes. Although he did not travel with de Soto, he sought to reconstruct events in elaborate detail; his highly romanticized account leaves out some of the grimmer

De Soto and his officers, on horseback, supervise the landing of troops in Florida in 1539. The horse, which is not native to the New World, was perhaps the Spaniards' most important resource and most valuable weapon in their conquests.

truths. The mestizo son of a Peruvian mother and Spanish father, Garcilaso interviewed one member of the expedition years after it ended and embellished that oral history with his own romantic vision of the dashing caballeros of Spain squaring off against the noble savages of the New World. According to Biedma, for instance, Vitachuco mustered about 350 warriors at Napituca. The Inca, on the other hand, describes a squadron of almost 10,000 Indians, "chosen people, valiant and well disposed," arrayed in feather headdresses 3 feet tall.

But all four authors agreed on the ferocity of the fight. Aware of the cavaliers' advantage when mounted, the natives fired first at the horses; de Soto's buckled almost at once, "with four arrows through the chest and four in the knees, two on each side," according to the Inca. A page dismounted and gave his steed to the commander. Like most conquistadores, de Soto's cavalry probably rode a la genita and carried their long lances overhand, ready for quick thrusts at the Indians on the ground. After the Spaniards had skewered 30 or 40, Vitachuco's braves retreated. Some vanished into the forest; others plunged into two

The typical Timucuan village was built with defense in mind, as this drawing by 16th-century French explorers of Florida shows. The village is surrounded by an oval wall made of logs about 10 to 12 feet high. Two sentry posts guard either end of a narrow entrance, which allowed only two people at a time to pass through. The chief's dwelling is in the middle, surrounded by those of the rest of the villagers.

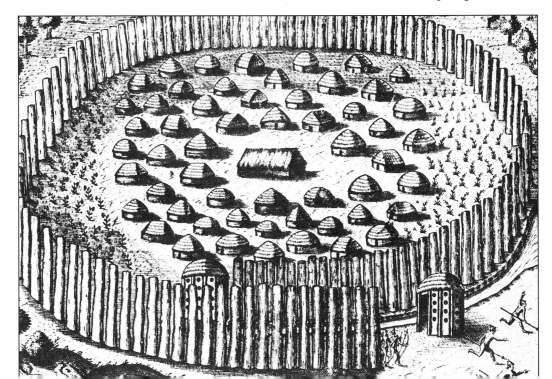

nearby lakes. The Spaniards encircled the lagoons and shot at the swimming warriors with their crossbows and harquebuses, but the Indians were too far away and the shots fell short. The Indians floated together in the deep water so that one archer at a time could climb upon his friends' backs and draw his bow. By evening, the Spaniards had given up on capturing the group in the larger lake and were concentrating on the 200 or so Indians in the smaller pond. From the banks, the soldiers continued to harass the fatigued swimmers, who tried to slip onto shore after dark by hiding under water lilies. At the slightest splash, Spanish riders spurred their horses into the water, driving back their quarry.

The standoff continued all night. Juan Ortiz and several Indian interpreters begged the swimmers to surrender. Most did, but there were 12 who preferred death to defeat. At four in the morning, Indian captives traveling with de Soto dove into the lake and dragged out the chilled and waterlogged survivors by their hair.

De Soto interrogated these warriors, who impressed him with their bravery and spirit. The 3 youngest, who were no older than 18, de Soto entertained and then sent home with "gifts of linens, silks, mirrors, and other things from Spain" as a gesture of friendship to their families. After threatening the remaining prisoners, including Vitachuco, the adelantado let them off with a lecture and a pardon of sorts: They were allowed to keep their lives, but as slaves in the service of the Spanish, who needed able bodies to carry their provisions on the march northwest to the province of Apalache, a recommended wintering spot. As a gesture of reconciliation, de Soto did order that Vitachuco be treated as a visiting dignitary, albeit a hostage one.

The triumph at Napituca invigorated the Spaniards. Ever since the Spanish had landed on the southwest coast of Florida in June, they had been bedeviled by Indians, who ambushed the invaders from behind trees. Guerrilla

(continued on page 20)

A

RELATION

OF THE

Invasion and Conquest

OF

FLORIDA

BY THE

S P A N I A R D S,

Under the Command of

FERNANDO de SOTO.

Written in Portuguese by a Gentleman of the Town of ELVAS.

Now ENGLISHED.

To which is Subjoyned Two Journeys of the present Emperour of CHINA into Tartary in the Years 1682, and 1683.

With some Discoveries made by the Spaniards in the Island of CALIFORNIA, in the Year 1683.

London: Printed for John Lawrence at the Angel in the Poultry over against the Compter. 1686.

One eyewitness account of de Soto's expedition in the New World was written by an unidentified Portuguese nobleman, the so-called Gentleman of Elvas. Elvas admired the strength and charisma of de Soto but was disgusted by his merciless mistreatment of the Native Americans.

Through the Eyes of the Inca

Writing history has much in common with solving crimes. Like a detective, a researcher sorts through the evidence to determine not only what happened at a certain place and time but also the motives of the people involved. Eyewitnesses provide crucial details, but their testimony may be misleading, skewed by fears, hopes, and biases. A careful historian weighs opposing viewpoints. Unfortunately, tracking down two sides of the story of the European discovery and settlement of North America has been difficult for scholars: As colonizers and colonists hounded Native Americans to near or total extinction, their oral tradition—their equivalent of diaries and journals—died with their storytellers. In the small library of primary sources about de Soto, *The Florida of the Inca*, Garcilaso de la Vega's history of the expedition, stands out for its extensive and sympathetic—although not entirely accurate—portrayal of the Indians of the southeastern United States.

As Garcilaso (1539–1616) wrote in his preface, he felt "under obligation to two races" and proud of both. He was born in Cuzco, Peru, the illegitimate but Catholic son of Chimpa Ocllo, an Indian princess, and Don Sebastián Garcilaso de la Vega y Vargas, a conquistador. In the New World, racial differences did not trouble Spaniards as much as religious differences, probably because of their tradition of intermarriage with Moors (Muslim Arabs) who had converted. For social and political reasons, conquistadores might not wed their Indian mistresses, but they often acknowledged their mestizo children. Garcilaso embraced both heritages.

After Don Sebastián died, the 20-year-old Inca—as Garcilaso later called himself—bid farewell to his mother and sailed to Spain to seek the money and recognition from the Crown that he felt was due his father. There, he joined the army and in 1568 helped the king's forces subdue a rebellion of Muslim converts. After his discharge, the Inca retired to Córdoba, where he increased his religious devotion and his literary output. Besides *The Florida of the Inca*, finished in 1599, he wrote an opus about the rise and fall of the Inca Empire, a translation of an Italian discourse about love, and a family history.

Although Garcilaso knew several survivors of the de Soto expedition, he derived his information from three sources—the moldy manuscripts of Juan Coles and Alonso de Carmona and a lengthy interview with an unidentified informant, whom historians have pinpointed as Gonzalo Silvestre. (Not surprisingly, Silvestre stars in the narrative.) In his account, the Inca faithfully documents the derring-do of the conquistadores, but he gives equal time to the natives, whose eloquent speeches he hoped would stir Spain to Christianize them. "Our elders have taught us," four of Vitachuco's braves confess to de Soto, "that the vanquished one who is faithful and who minimizes the value of his life for the honor of preserving the liberty of his country as well as his own personal liberty, deserves no less than the triumphant conqueror who uses his victory well."

The passion and poetry of the Inca has alarmed some scholars, who caution readers not to let charm blind them to some of the obviously fabricated details. Yet the truth of the work lies in its spirit, typical of the upbeat novels about military heroes popular in the 16th century. As John and Jeanette Varner point out in the introduction to their fine translation of *The Florida of the Inca*, "while adhering in general to what others have reported of geography and events, it reflects, in its very romanticism, the true heart and soul of those cavaliers who . . . set forth to brave unknown perils and explore mystic and pagan lands."

Garcilaso de la Vega.

(continued from page 17)

warfare disoriented the Europeans, who were accustomed to more choreographed battles. Their horses floundered in the marshes, and chest deep in slime, the infantry had trouble loading their cumbersome crossbows and 18-pound muskets. Although water afforded some protection, the soldiers detested the whizzing arrows that pinged against their brassards (elbow-to-shoulder covers), cuirasses (breast- and backplates), and light metal helmets with brims. Some barbs of fish bone or sharpened stone even penetrated this defensive armor, a uniform that the Spaniards had copied from the Swiss.

To guarantee the safe passage of his men through each territory, de Soto had adopted the habit of imprisoning the local *cacique* (the Caribbean word for chief, borrowed by the Spaniards) and releasing him and his people only after the expedition had passed into the domain of the next chieftain. In theory, the official policy of the Spanish crown prohibited de Soto from enslaving the natives. After much debate, scholars had decided that Indians qualified as rational human beings with souls and therefore could be converted to Catholicism through peaceful means— provided they renounced all their own beliefs and non-European customs. Twelve Dominican priests accompanied de Soto to spread the gospel. But the exigencies of the trek took precedence over the niceties of the law, and the adelantado relied upon Indian labor for everything from finding trails to washing clothes.

To the surprise of de Soto's men, many Indians did not cower before the might of Spain. When captured, the braves volunteered to act as guides but then led the army into quagmires. The Spaniards sicced their greyhounds on the uncooperative scouts, but even after the dogs had mauled them and their companions, the natives resisted de Soto's orders. Those soldiers who had served beside the adelantado in Mexico and Peru had learned firsthand about the diversity of Indian cultures in the New World, but the centralized civilizations of the Aztecs and the Incas

In the New World, the Spaniards used packs of dogs to help subdue the Indians, who were frequently hunted down by the ferocious hounds and eaten. Use of this tactic was so widespread that the Spanish coined a new verb, aperrear, *which meant to cast to the dogs.*

differed greatly from the multitude of loosely affiliated tribes in Florida, where subduing the natives was an endless struggle. At least in Napituca the Spaniards had finally fought on open ground—and won. Even though they still had no solid leads on the whereabouts of gold or silver, in Napituca they slept relatively comfortably in Indian lodges while the residents waited upon them.

In the role of magnanimous victor, de Soto invited Vitachuco to dine with him. Less than a week after the battle, at the end of dinner, the cacique yawned and stretched in sated satisfaction. Then, as the Inca describes it, "he shook his arms once or twice with such force and violence as to cause both bones and joints to crack like breaking canes." In an instant the chief leaped upon de Soto, seized him by the collar with his left hand, punched him in the face with his right, and "stretched him out unconscious on his back as if he had been a child." With a roar, Vitachuco fell upon de Soto to pummel him to death, but the stunned Spanish officers who had been eating with the adelantado recovered their wits, drew their swords, and stabbed the chief.

On cue, the cry of the thwarted murderer triggered a revolt throughout the camp. The slaves grabbed whatever was handy to strike at their masters—pestles, plates, jars, pitchers, benches, burning wood from the cook fires, pots of boiling water. Despite their manacles, the warriors managed to injure a few Spaniards. One beat his master with sticks and then held off a handful of soldiers with a lance until Diego de Soto, a distant cousin of the adelantado, shot him with a crossbow. Another brave climbed up onto a maize crib made of cane and menaced the crowd with a lance until a halberdier hurled a battle-ax at him. According to Elvas, the Spaniards had to overcome 200 rebellious captives.

The unusual weapons resorted to by the Indians inflicted painful wounds, including a great many broken noses and burned forearms. Unconscious for more than half an hour, de Soto bled from the eyes, nose, mouth, gums, and lips. His attacker had knocked out two teeth and loosened the rest, so for almost a month the adelantado had to suck soft food and apply plasters to his swollen nose and lips. The Spaniards were furious. Some lynched any Indian they could lay their hands on, while others turned their slaves over to de Soto, who awarded a few young ones to vigilant soldiers. The rest he left to the judgment of his guard, who tied the troublemakers to a post in the center of town.

At least one Indian anticipated that he would not get a fair trial—or any trial at all. According to the Inca, this individual seized his master, "a small and very neat person named Francisco de Saldana," by the seat of the trousers and tossed him headfirst into the ground, "then he jumped on him with his feet so angrily as to almost burst him open with his kicks." Nearby Spaniards rushed to the aid of their compatriot, but the desperate Indian, a leash probably still dangling from his neck, grabbed Saldana's sword and held the rescuers at bay by swinging it in an arc. The soldiers drew back but eventually killed him with long-handled weapons. Next, de Soto's men rounded up the Indians they had captured in the province of Paracoxi and ordered them to bombard the rebels with arrows. This would foil escape attempts, the Spaniards reasoned, for after the execution the Paracoxi Indians would hesitate to sneak away in the woods lest they meet Vitachuco's vengeful kinsmen. Finally, the uprising was quelled.

On September 23, the expedition set out for Apalache. As word of the massacre spread, Indians abandoned their villages along the Spaniards' route. De Soto ordered his men to antagonize the natives as little as necessary, but many of the Spaniards had vowed never to trust an Indian again. At the slightest provocation, they were ready to rob, rape, or kill.

When the captive chief Vitachuco attacked de Soto in a murderous frenzy, he sparked an uprising by the other Indian captives that the Spanish were hard pressed to subdue.

First Contacts

De Soto's soldiers were not the first explorers to ride roughshod over the natives of Florida. From Juan Ponce de León's discovery of the peninsula in 1513 to Pánfilo de Narváez's disastrous expedition along the Gulf Coast in 1527, the Spanish had been searching the mainland for gold and sites to colonize. Literally and figuratively, de Soto walked in the footsteps of these earlier conquistadores. His expedition benefited from the geographical data they had gathered, but it also harvested the ill will they had sown among Native Americans.

Born to a poor but distinguished family sometime around 1474, Juan Ponce de León as a boy served as a page to Pedro Nuñez de Guzmán, an influential figure at the Spanish court. As a young man, he joined other notable relatives as a soldier of the *Reconquista* (Reconquest), as the military crusade to drive the Moors from the Iberian Peninsula was known. In 1492, robust, ruddy-faced Ponce de León marched behind the militantly Catholic monarchs Ferdinand and Isabella into Granada, the last stronghold of Islam in Spain. Spain, which had been divided for centuries, was now united under the banners of Catholicism and the Crown, but decades of fighting had left the country devastated and impoverished. Many of its leading citizens had fallen into economic ruin in the course of years of military service. With few assets left other than

The Spanish charge into battle against the Moors, as the North African adherents of Islam who controlled varying portions of the Iberian Peninsula between the 7th and 15th centuries were known. The Reconquista, as the Spanish war to drive the Moors from Europe is known, left several generations of Spanish nobility battle hardened and eager for adventure in the New World.

Juan Ponce de León made a name for himself as a young man fighting the Moors in Spain. After Catholic forces succeeded in finally defeating the Moors in 1492, young noblemen were encouraged to seek their fortunes in the New World in lieu of pay, and Ponce de León signed on as a gentleman volunteer on Columbus's second voyage.

their honor and noble lineage, the aggressive *hidalgos* (noblemen) who helped Spain achieve victory over the Moors looked for their payoff in the New World.

Thanks to his connections, Ponce de León was able to sign on as a gentleman volunteer on Christopher Columbus's second voyage to the Indies in 1493. Leaving behind his young bride, Inez, in September he sailed with the 17-ship flotilla that departed from the southern seaport of Cádiz. Across the Atlantic, the fleet explored scores of islands in the Bahamas and called briefly at Añasco Bay in Puerto Rico before continuing on to the island of Hispaniola (today divided between Haiti and the Dominican Republic), where Columbus had left 44 well-provisioned settlers the year before, ensconced in a fortress, called Navidad, built from the timbers of his wrecked flagship, the *Santa Maria*.

No one rowed out to greet the admiral, however, and the thunder of his ship's guns was met only with silence. Eager to find a fortune in gold, unwilling to plant or hunt, desperate for companionship, the Spaniards at Navidad had pressed the Indians into service as slaves and stolen their women. The Indians quickly tired of this behavior and eventually slew their oppressors. Virtually from his first encounter with the people of the New World, Columbus had remarked on how timid, gentle, and trusting the Indians were and, consequently, on what a simple matter it would be to conquer and enslave them. Now, for the first time, the Spanish were made to realize that the character of the Indians was of a complexity to match their own, but except in a comparatively few individuals, this did not awaken a necessarily greater respect on the part of the Europeans. The Spanish learned little from the debacle at Navidad. As they set about establishing a new coastal city 30 miles east, Columbus was hard pressed to get any of his men to plant crops, which the Spanish disdained as a peasant task. Instead, to solve the labor problem, the Spanish instituted the *repartimiento* (later *encomienda*), a system of mutual responsibility (in theory) that exacted the labor of the Indians in mines or farms in exchange for the provision of basic needs and instruction in Christianity by landholders. Individual Spaniards were given large grants of land in the island's interior, which entitled them as well to the services of all the Indians living on "their" property. Although religious principles led Queen Isabella to oppose the enslavement of the Indians (King Ferdinand had fewer qualms and regarded the slave trade as yet another method to fill the royal coffers), in practice the repartimiento differed little from slavery, and under both forms of involuntary servitude Indians died in great numbers of disease, hunger, and overwork.

Death in battle also reduced their numbers. Spanish soldiers, hardened by years of warfare on their native peninsula, built forts and hunted down native rebels and runaway slaves, who hid in the hills and limestone caves at the fertile northeast end of the island, a province known as Higüey. Ponce de León and his officers subdued this outlaw region; for his efforts, he was appointed lieutenant to Nicolás de Ovando, who had replaced the autocratic Columbus as the island's governor.

Ponce de León's wife, son, and daughter soon joined him on Hispaniola, but before long an Indian bearing a huge nugget of gold excited his curiosity about Borinquén, as the Spanish sometimes called Puerto Rico. With Ovando's permission, in 1506 or 1508 he sailed over to the nearby island in a small caravel. Thanks to the cooperation of the local cacique (whose mother urged him to surrender), the red-haired conquistador subjugated the Taino Indians within a year. His business on Hispaniola completed, back in Spain Ovando regaled the king with the exploits of Ponce de León, whom Ferdinand promptly appointed governor of Puerto Rico.

After building a fortified capital, Villa de San German, near Añasco Bay, Ponce de León sent for his family, but he allowed himself little time to relax, for maintaining order demanded most of his energy and attention. For use in hunting down the many Indians who still actively opposed Spanish rule, he imported greyhounds, which the Spaniards had used to terrorize the natives of Hispaniola. Ponce de León's own dog, red-pelted, black-eyed Becerillo (Little Calf), became legendary for his ability to sniff out a single hostile native amidst a group of friends. The 16th-century historian Antonio de Herrera y Tordesillas reported that "the Indians were more afraid of 10 Spaniards with the dog, than of 100 without him." Becerillo proved so valuable that he earned for his master a crossbowman's pay as well as gold and slaves. In the New World the conquistadores coined a new verb, *aperrear*, which meant "to cast to the dogs."

Politics, not Indians, caused the greatest trouble for Ponce de León, whose savvy as an administrator did not match his mettle as a conquistador. His appointment on Puerto Rico had trespassed on the hereditary rights of Columbus's son Diego, who insisted upon placing his favorites in key posts in the Indies. Unfortunately for Ponce de León, he had once jailed Diego's two appointees for Puerto Rico, Juan Ceron and Miguel Dias de Aux. His squabbles with local dignitaries intensified, but the veteran warrior always managed to retain the king's favor: "See in which way you may best serve us over there," Ferdinand wrote him in July 1511.

Tales about an island called Bimini, where it was said there was a fountain whose waters restored vigor to aging men, piqued 38-year-old Ponce de León's curiosity. Although modern readers may regard the notion of a fountain of youth as outlandish, it should be remembered that myths about restorative waters existed in virtually every culture and that in his childhood Ponce de León had probably heard some version of this legend. Moreover, 16th-century European explorers were prepared, if not expecting, to encounter even the most fantastic wonders.

Columbus, for example, returned from his third expedition, on which he had reached the mouth of the Orinoco River in South America, convinced that he had sailed into the biblical Garden of Eden. But when filing for permission from the Crown to search for Bimini, Ponce de León listed more practical objectives than the discovery of a magical spring—new land and slaves.

On February 23, 1512, Ponce de León received approval for his mission. Like all such contracts, his contained explicit stipulations on everything from mineral rights to the distribution of land and Indians to the structure of future municipalities. Adelantado Ponce de León was granted civil and criminal jurisdiction over the new territory for the rest of his life, but he was expected to outfit the expedition at his own expense.

The *adelantamiento* was a system of licensed entrepreneurship that can be traced back to 12th-century Castile, a region of Spain and homeland to Isabella that had once been an independent kingdom. Adelantados first acted as magistrates, or agents of the king, but their powers expanded during the Moorish wars, when Spain's monarchs awarded rich frontier estates for loyal service. If a noble could defend the land, he could profit from it. In the New World, the system guaranteed maximum gain and minimum pain for the Crown. In return for certain incomes and monopolies, adelantados assumed the costs and risks of conquest and defense. Within a generation or two, titles and privileges reverted back to the monarchy.

Ponce de León departed from the Puerto Rican port of San German on March 3, 1513. Although the log of the expedition has been lost, Herrera consulted it when compiling his 16th-century account. Besides sailors, the adelantado recruited soldiers and a number of landsmen. At least one man, Francisco de Ortega, brought his wife, Beatriz Jiminez, who in turn was accompanied by her sister Juana.

Queen Isabella of Spain, whose religious principles led her to oppose the enslavement of Indians in the New World. Her husband, Ferdinand, was less troubled by the suggestions of Columbus and other explorers that the slave trade could be used to fill royal coffers.

Diego Bermudez, brother of the discoverer of the island of Bermuda, skippered the lead caravel *Santiago*, assisted by the 31-year-old chief pilot, Anton de Alaminos from Palos, the Andalusian port that had supplied the manpower for Columbus's first voyage. (Some scholars believe Alaminos had served as a ship's boy for Columbus.) Two Indians familiar with the Lucayas, as the Bahamas were known, also helped navigate. Juan Buono de Quexo, an old friend of Ponce de León, captained the triangular-sailed caravel *Santa Maria de Consolación*, and Juan Perez de Ortubia was at the helm of the two-masted brigantine *San Cristobal*. All but the last belonged to the adelantado. He had ordered the brigantine, like the other ships, from Spain, but since it did not arrive in time, he requisitioned one that usually ferried between Puerto Rico and Hispaniola.

The ships set a northwest course. In one day less than a month, after skirting the Caicos and Turks Islands, stopping briefly at Guanahani (San Salvador), Columbus's first

This 16th-century engraving of the first encounter between Native Americans and Europeans on the Florida coast is based on the famous work of Theodore de Bry, a Flemish artist whose portrayals of New World subjects won him great popularity. Ponce de León is generally credited with being the European discoverer of Florida.

landing spot in the Indies, and sighting Great Abaco Island, the fleet anchored in eight fathoms of water off a previously uncharted coast. The next day, the adelantado rowed ashore to take possession of this region for Spain. Lush groves of grey cypress, tulip, ash, and magnolia trees, backed by tall palms and broom pines, exuded a delightful bouquet. Azaleas, oranges, and jasmines were in bloom, and the woods were alive with the drones and squawks of insects, hummingbirds, loons, and wild turkeys. Because Ponce de León had made his discovery on the Catholic feast day of Pascua Florida (the Easter of Flowers), he called the new land Florida. (Like many explorers in years to come, Ponce de León believed Florida to be an island.) Using an astrolabe, the forerunner of the sextant, to compute the altitude of the stars, the fleet's navigators had determined the ships' position to be about 30 degrees north latitude. A faulty instrument or out-of-date tables probably distorted that reading, however, and most scholars place Ponce de León's landfall somewhere farther south, between what are now Daytona Beach and New Smyrna Beach on the east coast.

On April 8, the three ships set sail once again, to the north at first, just briefly, then south following the shore. Two weeks later, the Spaniards spotted some huts, the first sign they had seen of Indians. The next day they encountered a current strong enough to offset the favorable wind that filled their sails. When the two ships closest to shore dropped anchor, they strained at their moorings; the brigantine, unable to resist the current's force, drifted out to sea and was lost to its sister vessels for two days. Although Ponce de León had no way of knowing it at the time, this current—the Gulf Stream—was as important a find as Florida. From its origins in the Gulf of Mexico, the stream passes through the Straits of Florida and shoots up the southeastern United States coast until it meets a cold current off Cape Hatteras, North Carolina, and then flows northeast into the Atlantic Ocean. Years later, Alaminos charted a course for cargo vessels bound for Spain that used the 50-foot-wide current, which averages a speed of 4 miles per hour, to speed them on their way.

For the present, the conquistador and explorer was more interested in the Indians who had appeared and were motioning him ashore, but when he complied the Indians wounded two of his men with bone-tipped arrows and tried to seize his longboat. The Spaniards retreated and sailed south to a river that was probably somewhere near Jupiter Inlet. While they gathered wood and water and waited for the *San Cristobal*, another party of Indians attacked. This time the explorers fared a little better in the skirmish, and Ponce de León captured one of the Indians to train as an interpreter and guide.

On Sunday, May 8, the ships rounded the Florida cape, which Ponce de León named Cabo de las Corrientos (Cape of the Currents) after the forceful current. The next week they passed a string of small islands, which they dubbed Los Martires (the Martyrs) because the rocks resembled suffering men. Navigating the shallow waters around the keys taxed Alaminos; to avoid running aground, he posted a lookout for changes in water color and heaved the sounding lead over the side to check the depth. At night even such careful navigation was impossible, and the ships had to anchor.

In the Marquesas Keys, Calusa Indians wearing palm-leaf loincloths canoed across an inlet to trade animal pelts and guanin, a low-grade gold. To the great surprise of the crew, one of them spoke Spanish, taught to him either by slave traders or by shipwrecked sailors. When the bargaining soured, the natives seized the anchor cable of one of the ships and tried to tow it away. In the ensuing struggle, the Spaniards captured four Indian women, who indicated that a chief named Carlos had gold to sell. Following the captives' directions, the explorers steered north up the west coast to Charlotte Harbor. On June 11, Carlos greeted the Spaniards, but with 80 canoes of arch-

ers, not precious metals. Neither side, however, got close enough to inflict injury on the other.

Three days later, having had no luck in finding gold, Ponce de León ordered his fleet to turn around. The ships veered west to the Dry Tortugas, where the men, dazzled by the abundant wildlife, killed 160 giant sea turtles, numerous seals and manatees, and thousands of gannets and pelicans. Trying to follow the directions of an Indian captive, the commander directed the flotilla east. In the Bahamas once more, the untrustworthy *San Cristobal* foundered, but the men of the other two ships managed to rescue its crew.

Although the explorers had sipped sweet water from a spring on Key Biscayne, Ponce de León had not succeeded

As Europeans watch the proceeding, some Timucuan Indians conduct a tribal council. According to French explorers who visited the region in the late 16th century, the potion the Indian women at lower right are ladling out is an extremely strong herb tea, which each participant in the council was required to imbibe. Those who could not stomach the brew were never entrusted with military or serious responsibilities.

in locating his rejuvenating fountain. He decided to head home in the *Santiago* but instructed Ortubia and Alaminos to continue the search in the *Santa Maria*. On October 10, 1513, a little more than seven months after he had left, Ponce de León returned to Puerto Rico. His scouts returned in February, having discovered the island of Bimini but not the wellspring of youth.

To prevent any rivals—particularly those working for the Columbus clan—from claiming his achievements as their own, Ponce de León sailed for Spain in early 1514. He presented the king with 5,000 gold pesos (which came from his personal coffers, not his travels) and received a grant to colonize the islands of Bimini and Florida, but pressing business in the Caribbean delayed the start of his next venture. First, he led a campaign against the warlike Carib Indians, who had been launching raids from the Lesser Antilles. Next, he masterminded the move of the Puerto Rican capital to a more convenient site on the island's northern coast, where the new city of San Juan was founded. Finally, in February 1521, he set out to domesticate Florida.

On this second voyage, Ponce de León stocked his ships with seeds, horses, and livestock, all essential for the establishment of a permanent settlement, and enlisted priests to attend to the spiritual needs of the colonists and establish missions for the conversion of the Indians. Somewhere on the west coast, perhaps on Sanibel Island, Ponce de León and his 200 men began constructing a settlement, but disease and Indians quickly thinned their ranks. Although Europeans who later visited the region reported the natives to be friendly, the veteran conquistador was in the habit of using strong-arm diplomacy, and the Indians responded in kind. In the course of one of many battles between the uninvited newcomers and the inhabitants, an arrow wounded Ponce de León in the thigh. Infection set in, and although his men shipped him off to Havana, Cuba, for treatment, there was little that could be done. He died there in July 1521.

In his own century, advocates for the Indians, such as the priest and historian Bartolomé de Las Casas, reviled Ponce de León as a villain, but others, such as the poet Juan de Castellanos, praised him: "In every gesture strong and full of grace/Hard tasks begun, he carried to the end." The epitaph on his tomb read "Here rest the bones of a Lion/mightier in deeds than in name." Certainly, Ponce de León possessed the courage of a lion, as well as unusual energy and ambition that enabled him to play an instrumental role in establishing European civilization in the New World. Yet, like so many European explorers before and after him, he possessed little appreciation for the inherent value of the civilizations already established in the Americas by the continents' original inhabitants and thus contributed to the series of perhaps inevitable tragedies that would devastate the native peoples of the New World.

Slavers and Sailors

In between Ponce de León's two journeys, other ambitious traders and explorers visited Florida. From Cuba, pilot Diego Miruelo sailed up the west coast of the peninsula in 1516, in the process discovering a bay (probably Pensacola) and bartering with friendly Indians. On Cuba, as elsewhere, the Spanish oppression had severely reduced the native population, so in 1517 two caravels and a brigantine commanded by Hernandez de Cordóba and the sea-wise Alaminos sailed from there in search of slaves. The well-armed party landed on the Yucatán Peninsula, where the Mayans must have been suspicious of their uninvited guests' intentions, for these usually peaceable inhabitants of the region ambushed the Spaniards. Only half of the Spanish expedition escaped with their lives, and most of the survivors were wounded.

According to the priest and historian Bartolomé de Las Casas, who chronicled the excesses of the Spanish in the New World, the hunting of Indians for sport by Spaniards on horseback was among the atrocities committed. Swift greyhounds joined in the chase.

In search of a safe haven and fresh water, Alaminos directed the three ships across the gulf to a bay in southwest Florida. Ashore, while he and a colleague supervised 20 of the healthiest soldiers in digging wells, the local Indians, probably furious over Ponce de León's earlier raids, attacked in canoes and on foot. "They had very large bows and good arrows and lances and a sort of sword, and were dressed in deerskins," a survivor remembered. Waist deep in water, the Spaniards fought back with crossbows and swords, killing 32 of the enemy, but the Indians captured the Spanish sentry and wounded 6 others. The Europeans beat a hasty retreat to their ships; back in Havana, Hernandez de Cordóba and many of the battered crew succumbed to their wounds and died.

Despite this debacle, slavers continued to ply the waters around Florida. Lucas Vazquez de Ayllón, an official from Hispaniola, oversaw forays along the east coast of the peninsula in the 1520s. Still hopeful that someone would stumble upon a western sea passage to the Spice Islands, for which Columbus had been searching, King Charles, Ferdinand's grandson and successor, authorized Vazquez de Ayllón's colonization of the province of Chicora, in present-day South Carolina. His expedition explored the eastern coast of Florida and points north in 1526, but back-to-back shipwrecks left it desperately short of food and other necessary provisions and its Indian guides ran away. Lost and hungry, the would-be colonists attempted to establish a settlement near Savannah, Georgia, but despite the abundance of game and vegetation in the region, the Spaniards proved unable to fend for themselves. After Vazquez de Ayllón died in October, dissension destroyed morale, and scores began to succumb to illness and starvation. Finally, 150 sickly men and women, less than one-third of the expedition's original complement, managed to drag themselves out of the forest and head for home, but on the return voyage 7 of the ill-clad survivors froze to death, including one frostbite victim who pulled all the flesh off his shins.

The most notable discovery of this period belonged to Alvarez de Pineda, who conducted some of his voyages of exploration on behalf of the wealthy lieutenant governor of Jamaica, Francisco de Garay. In March 1519, Garay dispatched Pineda, 270 men, and 4 vessels to locate the passage believed to separate the "island" of Florida from the mainland. Pineda and his pilots, among them the ubiquitous Alaminos, failed, of course, but they did trace the peninsula's shoreline as far to the southwest as Mexico. After the expedition, the pilots mapped the entire Gulf of Mexico in roughly accurate proportions and correctly labeled Florida a peninsula. Although historians have questioned some of Pineda's reports from this expedition—he claimed to have encountered giants and dwarfs, for example—most credit his assertion that he meandered into the mouth of a great river, known today as the Mississippi.

Shipwreck and Survival

Like Garay, Pánfilo de Narváez, already a rich man thanks to his wife's astute management of the fortune he had pillaged as a conquistador, aspired to the power and glory of discovery for the empire. His intellect, however, was not as deep as his pocketbook; historian Samuel Eliot Morison calls him "the most incompetent of all who sailed for Spain in this era." Friends who tried to dissuade the one-eyed hidalgo from undertaking a venture as risky as a voyage of exploration found that they were wasting their breath, and with the permission of King Charles, he assembled at Havana 5 ships and 600 people for the purpose of colonizing the countryside between Rio de Las Palmas in Mexico and the cape of Florida.

Despite Narváez's enthusiasm, several complications delayed his departure. Because so many Spanish settlers in the Caribbean had discovered that gold was not as easy to find there as Columbus and others had advertised and had accordingly abandoned the islands in favor of Mexico and Peru, the Council of the Indies, the royal advisory board, had outlawed this emigration, making it necessary for Narváez to staff his expedition largely with Old World residents of Castile. Then, when he sent his treasurer and high sheriff Alvar Núñez Cabeza de Vaca to load supplies in Trinidad in the autumn of 1527, this otherwise praiseworthy lieutenant, through no fault of his own, lost 2 ships, 60 men, and 20 horses in a ferocious hurricane. Narváez hurried to Trinidad to wait out the winter with the terrified survivors there, but as he attempted to bring his fleet back to Havana the following spring, he managed to run several of the vessels aground. At sea once again, the beleaguered fleet was battered by another tempest, which drove the ships before it all the way to a shallow bay on the southwest coast of Florida.

A Timucuan Indian village bordered this inlet, but by the time Narváez rowed in from the anchorage, the natives had fled, leaving behind only fishnets and a gold rattle. Still, this trinket was enough to inflame the gold-lust of any would-be conquistador, and the explorers' hopes were duly whetted, their travails quickly forgotten. On April 18, 1528, Narváez took possession of the territory with all the requisite ceremony. As required by Spanish law, he recited the *requerimiento* for the benefit of the Indians, even though none were present. In Latin, he delivered to the village's enormous empty lodge the standard summary of the history of the Catholic church, of Pope Alexander VI's division of the New World between Spain and Portugal, and of the requirement that Indians obey the pope and king and accept the preaching of Christianity. If the Native Americans resisted, Narváez warned:

> I will take the persons of yourselves, your wives and your children to make slaves, sell and dispose of you . . . and I will take your goods, doing you all the evil and injury that I may be able . . . and I declare to you that the deaths

Pope Alexander VI, who in 1494 proclaimed the Treaty of Tordesillas, which divided the New World between Portugal and Spain. At the time of the treaty, neither nation was particularly concerned with colonization or economic exploitation of the New World but rather with securing trade routes to the spice-rich Indies,

and damages that arise therefrom, will be your fault and not that of his Majesty, nor mine, nor of these cavaliers who came with me.

The commander's officers and notary duly witnessed that proper procedure had been followed.

Already short of supplies, with half their horses dead from the voyage, the Spaniards searched the immediate area for food and treasure. They found fields of maize but no ripe grain. In one village, they stumbled upon some Castilian merchandise crates containing European corpses in deerskins—most likely the victims of a shipwreck. Whenever the Spaniards did manage to corner some Indians, the soldiers flashed gold, eager for directions to a mother lode. Always, they received the same answer: Apalache.

This information was enough for Narváez, who decided to abandon his ships and march overland for that province. The brigantine had already sailed on ahead; pilot Diego Miruelo (probably the same Diego Miruelo who had visited the Florida coast more than a decade earlier) claimed to remember a harbor to the north. Now Narváez wanted the other three ships (and the few women who had accompanied their husbands) to follow—against the advice of Cabeza de Vaca, who wrote down and notarized his objections. As it turned out, the levelheaded treasurer was right in his prediction that Narváez would never see his vessels again.

Although the trio of ships did discover Tampa Bay near the original anchorage, it hunted in vain for Miruelo's harbor. After scouring the coast for signs of Narváez and his overland party for a year without success, the ships and their crew headed for the safety of New Spain. Meanwhile, the crew of the brigantine rounded up reinforcements in Cuba and headed for the original landing site in Florida, where, of course, Narváez's company was no longer to be found. To make matters worse, Narváez had so enraged the cacique Hirrihigua—the Spaniard's crimes included

cutting off the cacique's nose and throwing his mother to the dogs—that the chief immediately imprisoned the four members of the brigantine's shore party. Helpless, the crew abandoned its comrades and sailed away.

In the meantime, Narváez's 300 men, only 40 of whom had horses, trekked northward. As a supplement to their meager rations of hardtack (unleavened bread made of flour and water) and salt pork, they munched on the leaves of dwarf palms. After crossing the Withlacoochee River on improvised rafts, they seized several Indians as path-finders and appropriated some corn from a local village. Near the Suwannee River, the wayfarers met up with a Timucuan chief in a painted deerskin riding on the shoul-ders of one of his subjects, surrounded by an entourage playing reed flutes. He invited the Spaniards home with

Timucuan archers fire arrows tipped with flaming moss at an enemy village. Some of the archers wear leather guards on their wrists to protect their forearms from their bowstrings. The Florida Indians' prowess with the bow and arrow amazed and frightened the Spaniards.

him, but their loutish behavior soon convinced him to abandon them to their own devices. Unabashed, the explorers simply impressed a few more natives as guides, who led them through the dense forests of north central Florida. In June, exasperated from clambering over trees felled as defensive barricades, they roared into Apalache, an unimpressive town of about 40 dwellings not far from present-day Tallahassee on the banks of Lake Miccasukee. Characteristically diplomatic, Narváez's hungry men immediately seized as hostages some of the village's women and children, earning themselves, for the next 25 days, a virtually unceasing storm of arrows from the expert Apalache archers, who wielded 6-foot bows hewn out of oak.

Word of ample maize, beans, and squash in a village not far from the sea—perhaps disinformation planted by a hostage Apalache—finally spurred Narváez to march his charges about 100 miles west over the pine-forested sand plain to the settlement of Aute. According to Cabeza de Vaca, the Apalache bowmen harassed the company for much of the way, shooting from concealed positions until they finally ran out of arrows. The Indians were obviously analyzing the Spaniards' armor, for they killed one hidalgo with a carefully placed shaft to the neck, just above the cuirass. The forewarned inhabitants of Aute had fled, after burning their huts to the ground, but their crops were still ripening in the fields. While most of the men rested, Narváez put the enterprising Cabeza de Vaca in charge of blazing a trail to the sea.

Cabeza de Vaca's scouting report, delivered upon his return, did not cheer his compatriots. The Apalache were regrouping behind the explorers, many creeks and bays lay between Aute and the gulf, and there had been no sign of the ships. On the move, the situation worsened. As the unwieldy column of men and horses tramped toward the gulf, Narváez and a third of the company came down with malaria, contracted from the voracious mosquitos at Aute, and the disgruntled cavalry, reasoning that

A wolf picks clean the bones of a member of the disastrous expedition of Pánfilo de Narváez. Despite the loss of his ships and a lack of supplies, Narváez led his men on a wild goose chase through north central Florida in search of gold. His plan to sail back to Mexico in jerry-built boats was doomed by lack of water, Indian ambushes, and a storm that wrecked all but one vessel of the slipshod flotilla.

they could travel much farther without the burden of an infantry, threatened to desert their fever-stricken comrades. At a bay on the coast, desperation gave birth to an imaginative if unlikely plan: Because the ships could not be located, the explorers would escape to Mexico in boats they would build themselves.

Construction of seaworthy vessels proved a singularly daunting task. With characteristic foresight, Narváez had enlisted no shipbuilders and only one carpenter. The Spaniards had no tools, no tar, no sails, no rope, and little food but plenty of ingenuity. They jerry-rigged a forge with bellows of hollow logs and deerskins; on it, they wrought their iron stirrups, spurs, and crossbows into nails, saws, and axes to transform tree trunks into planks and cypress logs into oars. While a Greek member of the expedition, Doroteo Teodoro, made water-resistant pitch from longleaf pines, others lined and caulked the wooden vessels with palm fibers. Every third day, a horse was sacrificed to feed the workers, who then tanned its hide for water bags and wove hair from its mane and tail into ropes. In honor of these selfless steeds, the Spaniards named the inlet Bahia de Caballos (Bay of Horses). In six weeks, by the end of September, Narváez's men had fashioned five crude boats, which flew sails made from shirts. After butchering and eating the last remaining horse, the 240 survivors—more than 50 men had been killed by the Indians or had died of hunger or disease—crowded onto their clumsy crafts and floated out into the coastal marshes.

Although seawater lapped just below the gunwales, thirst tormented the voyagers as they drifted westward. The leather water containers rotted, and while the boats waited out a storm in an island cove, five Spaniards died from drinking brine. Not long afterward, they docked at an Indian village where earthenware jugs of fresh water stood outside mat-roofed huts and a hospitable chief invited them to a lavish fish dinner, but later that same night they were ambushed, and Narváez and some others were wounded. The reluctant seafarers pushed off in the morning, but in just a few days the need for fresh water again drove them ashore, this time in the region of Mobile Bay, where Teodoro, the resin maker, and a black expeditioner made the mistake of following some Choctaw Indians to a spring. The two were never heard from again. More than a decade later, de Soto found the Greek's dagger and heard an Indian tell of their death.

By the end of October, the bedraggled Narváez expedition had reached the Mississippi River, where the powerful current separated the boats as it carried them out into the gulf. Two were swept away; to Cabeza de Vaca's plea for a towline, selfish Narváez, with the least-flimsy craft and the strongest crew, responded that "each should do what seemed best, which was to save his own life, which is what he intended to do. And saying thus, he pulled away."

Barely subsisting on handfuls of raw corn, Cabeza de Vaca's limp crew washed ashore on an island off the east Texas coast, near present-day Galveston, which they nicknamed Malhado (Misfortune). Kindly clans of Capoque and Han Indians welcomed the castaways and warmed them by fires, but their meager stores of roots could not support the strangers through the winter, and some of the Spaniards horrified the Indians by resorting to cannibalism. Yet when an epidemic ravaged the Indians, they begged the Spanish to treat the stricken, hoping that the newcomers possessed medicine unknown to them. Cabeza de Vaca and his 14 surviving compatriots had only their prayers to offer, but their entreaties worked, and many of the Indians recovered.

The Spanish now found themselves revered as powerful medicine men, and when Cabeza de Vaca, determined to leave "this country, so remote and malign, so destitute of all resource," set out west across the vast unknown, he found that news of his supposed powers preceded him to the various Indian villages along his route, where he was usually welcomed and treated well. In 1534, he met up with three survivors of the wreck of Narváez's ship—Andres Dorantos, Castillo, and Estevanico (a black Moroccan). Together this quartet walked more than 1,200 miles, crossing wind-scoured deserts, traversing the rugged Sierra Madre mountain range, and fording the Colorado, Brazos, Pecos, and Sonora rivers before reaching the Gulf of California.

Published five years after his triumphant return to Spain in 1537, Cabeza de Vaca's chronicle of the Narváez expedition and the survivors' ordeal in Texas stands as a classic of adventure and anthropology. Although he wrote frankly of hunger, heartache, fatigue, barren plains, hostile Indians, and all the other travails of his strange odyssey, it was the excitement of his reappearance, not the cautionary elements of his account, that captured the public imagination. In Spain, after Cabeza de Vaca's return, it seemed that every voyage to the New World unveiled new windows of opportunity and adventure, and that just a handful of turquoise and a bison hide—the type of trade goods Cabeza de Vaca exchanged with the Indians—were enough to compel a man to seek his destiny in the Americas.

Alvar Núñez Cabeza de Vaca leads the survivors of the Narváez expedition on a 1,200-mile journey through the American Southwest. In all likelihood, Cabeza de Vaca was the first European to cross the North American continent.

The Conquest Mentality

Like Ponce de León, Hernando de Soto inherited more honor than wealth with his noble pedigree. He was born in about 1500 in Jerez de los Caballeros in mountainous central Spain. In his youth, shipments of sugar, cotton, wood, herbs, hides, and gold from the Indies set the local countryside abuzz with stories of promise and possibility across the Atlantic. At the age of 14, de Soto sailed for the New World with his aging patron, Pedro Arias Dávila, whom the king had appointed governor of Darien, on the tropical Isthmus of Panama. There, just a year earlier, Vasco Núñez de Balboa (also from Jerez) had discovered the great South Sea—the Pacific Ocean.

As a protégé of the harsh Arias Dávila—who had Balboa executed for earlier treasonous activity—de Soto earned a reputation for boldness, stubbornness, and bravery. He also earned gold and Indian slaves as plunder from raids. As an insurance policy against future spells of bad luck, he signed two long-term partnership agreements with comrades-in-arms under which the trio of daring young conquistadores agreed always to divvy up their plundered loot.

But fortune seemed to bless the young captain. In 1523, de Soto served as an officer under Francisco Fernández de Cordóba, who had been sent by Arias Dávila to displace a rival in Nicaragua. Instead, Cordóba decided to take control of the province himself—an act of treason that de Soto opposed. Although he despised the cruelty and jealousy of Old Fury, as the men referred to Arias Dávila

Charles I of Spain authorized de Soto to "conquer, pacify, and populate" Florida. At the time, Charles ruled virtually half of Europe and controlled a vast, wealthy empire in the New World.

behind his back, de Soto would not betray his benefactor, who was, moreover, the legally empowered representative of the king. Cordóba had him imprisoned in the fortress of Granada, but he was soon sprung from jail by his friend and partner Francisco Companon. With eight like-minded companions, de Soto disappeared into the jungle and made his way back to Darien, where he delivered a full report to Arias Dávila. Old Fury then marched on Nicaragua, overthrew Cordóba, and had him drawn and quartered—the traditional Spanish method of punishment for traitors.

Over the course of the next several decades, Spain continued to expand its holdings in the New World. In 1519, an indomitable Spanish warrior named Hernán Cortés landed in Mexico on the west coast of the Bay of Campeche, where he founded the city of Veracruz. Then, after burning his ships so that there could be no turning back, he led his 500 men and 16 horses on a march westward to Tenochtitlán (on the site of present-day Mexico City), the capital city of the Aztecs, whose empire roughly matched Spain in population (10 million) and outshone it in resources. Through luck and canny exploitation of

The atrocities committed by the Spanish conquistadores are graphically and imaginatively illustrated in this 16th-century engraving. The Spaniards cut down tree houses where the Indians lived (left); soldiers on horseback herd Indians into a ditch, where they are impaled on sharp sticks (lower right); dogs and birds pick at dead bodies (center); a city in shambles at the foot of volcanoes erupting in Guatemala (upper middle and right).

The death of Aztec leader Montezuma II, who was stoned to death by his own people for his perceived cooperation with the Spanish invaders. The successful conquest of the Aztecs in Mexico by Hernán Cortés in the 1520s paved the way for later Spanish conquistadores such as Francisco Pizarro, who took Peru from the Incas, and de Soto.

the dissatisfaction of the subject peoples of the Aztecs, Cortés was able to prevail. By 1530, the Spanish had found and seized the great silver mines west of Mexico City, the first of many such strikes in Central and South America. Over the next few decades, the Mexican conquest alone netted Spain roughly $10 million in gold and $60 million in silver, fantastic sums in an age when a gallon of wine cost 8 cents, a seaman earned $26 a year, and $100,000 was enough to raise and outfit an army.

Cortés's triumphant visit to court in 1528 eased the way for Francisco Pizarro, a 52-year-old explorer who had returned to Spain to obtain a royal license for a foray into Peru. The illegitimate, illiterate son of a farmer, Pizarro had nevertheless made a successful career in the army. As a 35-year-old captain, he had bushwhacked to the Pacific with Balboa and had later launched several expeditions down the coast. In 1527, ships commanded by his partner, Diego de Almagro, captured a raft bearing gold crowns, silver bracelets, embroidered tunics, emeralds, beads, and more. These handicrafts hinted at the refinement of the civilization that produced them, but the Spanish were more interested in them as indications of vast wealth. Further contacts indicated that Peru was indeed home to a remarkably sophisticated civilization, notable for, among many things, advances in irrigation techniques, medicine, architecture, and astronomy. The empire of the Inca extended for more than 2,000 miles along South America's west coast, from present-day Ecuador all the way south to Chile. Emboldened by the success of Cortés, Pizarro proposed to conquer this civilization with an invasion force of 180 men.

In 1530, Hernando de Soto bought a captaincy in Pizarro's army. The Spaniards landed at Tumbes, on the Gulf of Guayaquil in present-day Ecuador, in January 1531, then moved overland through the lush Piura Valley, past the barren Sechura Desert, and into the forbidding Andes Mountains. They were in search of the city of

Cajamarca, where the new Inca (the ruler's title as well as name of the people) was said to have made his capital. To the advantage of the Spaniards, disease (perhaps smallpox, introduced by the Europeans) had recently killed the former ruler, decimated his court, and set his two sons battling for succession. As Cortés had in Mexico, Pizarro planned to use this unrest to his own advantage.

Finally, in the autumn of 1532, the Spaniards reached Cajamarca, which lay, according to one of its conquerors, "like a sparkling gem on the dark skirts of the sierra." Treacherously, Pizarro approached the rulers with respect, sending de Soto and 15 cavalry officers as his emissaries to the palace of Atahuallpa, on the outskirts of the city. (Atahuallpa had recently defeated, dethroned, and drowned Huáscar, his half brother and rival for the throne.) These delegates found the ruler relaxing in his bathhouse above a hot spring, sitting on a stool, surrounded by his harem. Like most of the Inca nobility, he wore a series of cords wrapped around his head, with a special tassel over his forehead as a sign of his rank. Aware that horses, which are not native to the New World, generally intimidated Indians, de Soto rode so close to the

De Soto displays his equestrian skills before Atahuallpa, the Inca. Having never seen a horse before, the king was fascinated by its swift, graceful movements, but he severely reproved members of his court who showed their fear of de Soto's steed.

Inca that the breath of his mount stirred the fringe on the ruler's headdress, but Atahuallpa did not flinch. Later, after presenting the Peruvian leader with a ring of friendship, de Soto gave a display of his equestrian skills, which was reported on by one of his fellow conquistadores:

> The nag was spirited and made much foam at its mouth. [The Inca] was amazed at this, and at seeing the agility with which it wheeled. But the common people showed even greater admiration and there was much whispering. One squadron of troops drew back when they saw the horse coming towards them. Those who did this paid for it that night with their lives, for Atahuallpa ordered them to be killed because they had shown fear.

De Soto meets Atahuallpa at the Inca's court in Cajamarca. The Spaniards were no less astounded by Atahuallpa's dignified bearing than they were by the prosperity of the Inca Empire.

Atahuallpa promised to meet Pizarro the next day in Cajamarca, but the Spaniard had not planned a diplomatic encounter. When bearers carried the unsuspecting Inca's litter into town the next evening for the arranged meeting, Spanish soldiers emerged from their hiding places and kidnapped the ruler, then slaughtered thousands of un-

armed Indians in the two hours before dark. Their corpses filled the city square, transforming the capital, in the words of one historian, into a city of the dead.

For a while, the Spaniards were willing to keep Atahuallpa alive, for their royal hostage protected them from attack and bought them time to summon reinforcements. Besides, the Inca offered—or was made to offer—a literal king's ransom for his life: a room 22 feet long by 17 feet wide filled to a height of 8 feet with gold, with twice that amount in silver.

Although Atahuallpa honored his bargain and the Spanish were soon busy melting down llama-loads of exquisitely wrought gold ornaments, Pizarro would not release the Inca. The commander and officers disagreed about what to do with their prisoner, with whom they had dined and played chess during the last eight months. De Soto, among others, argued against killing the Inca; if no longer useful as a hostage, he could be exiled to Spain. When rumors circulated that the Inca's forces were planning a rescue, Pizarro sent de Soto and four other horsemen to investigate. While they were gone, on the night of July 26, 1533, the remaining garrison baptized Atahuallpa and then had him strangled by some black slaves in the square of Cajamarca.

With Cajamarca subdued, Pizarro, de Soto, and the rest set off for Cuzco, a city of 200,000 people located several hundred miles south along the royal road, the remarkable highway the Incas had constructed thousands of feet above sea level amidst the precipitous defiles of the Andes. In Cuzco, as in Cajamarca, the Spaniards met little resistance and quickly sacked the city.

Several factors enabled the Spanish to prevail despite their having to fight on unfamiliar terrain, several thousand miles from home, at such a severe numerical disadvantage. Few historians will dispute that the Spanish were the foremost soldiers of 16th-century Europe, hardened by generations of conflict in their homeland. They

A 16th-century engraving of Atahuallpa. When he agreed to a meeting with Pizarro he unwittingly fell into a trap and was held for ransom while thousands of his people were slain. Later, he was strangled to death in the central square of Cajamarca.

were well equipped with armor, pikes, spears, and har-quebuses. Economic upheaval at home provided strong motivation to seek plunder abroad, while a militant Ca-tholicism enabled the Spanish to believe that in con-quering unbelievers they were doing God's work. Constant warfare had bred the Spanish for hardship. As Alan Lloyd writes in *The Spanish Centuries*, stubbornness, sobriety, and a "profound sense of superiority . . . inherited from the reconquest" enabled the tough recruits to endure "the utmost frugality in grueling climatic conditions."

But perhaps the greatest physical and psychological edge owned by the Spanish in Peru and elsewhere in the Amer-icas was the horse. The historian John Hemming called them the "tanks of the Conquest." In addition to simply terrifying the inhabitants of the New World, horses gave the Spanish an incomparable advantage in maneuvera-bility. In both Mexico and Peru, these steeds helped the Spanish take advantage of the mythology of the native peoples. The sight of these exotic newcomers, with their strange garb (armor), long sticks that could belch fire (guns), and prancing, powerful mounts convinced both the Aztecs and the Incas that the Spanish were gods. Ac-cording to Atahuallpa's nephew, the Incas called the strangers *viracochas*, an ancient name for their creator, because they sported different colored beards, conveyed messages on white sheets, fired weapons of thunder, and "because we saw that they rode on enormous animals that had feet of silver—we said silver because of the shine of the horses' shoes."

Among the conquistadores, caballeros also commanded awe—and pocketed a larger share of the spoils. De Soto's portion of the Inca's ransom, for instance, was 180 pounds of gold and 360 pounds of silver, and each new campaign swelled his coffers. For a time, he served as lieutenant governor in Cuzco, where he fathered a daughter by an Indian mistress, but he soon grew tired of the constant political squabbles between Pizarro and de Almagro. In

1536, he returned to Spain, where he was greeted as a hero because of his courage and affluence.

With some of his 180,000 *cruzados*, de Soto established a lavish household in Seville, hiring an equerry (horse attendant), a chamberlain, footmen, pages, and all the other servants befitting a gentleman. He also married Isabel de Bobadilla, daughter of his late patron, Arias Dávila, but domestic life could not long hold his attention, especially once a sizable loan he made to the Crown gained him an invitation to the court. Three colleagues from Peru—Luis Moscoso de Alvarado, Nuño de Tobar, and Juan Rodriguez Lobillo—as well as other kith and kin accompanied de Soto to his first audience with the king. "They went well and costly apparelled," the Gentleman of Elvas reported, "and Soto, although by nature not profuse, spent largely."

Pizarro enters the city of Cuzco in 1533. His forces met little resistance from the population of about 200,000, and it fell as easily as Cajamarca before it.

The conquistador asked the king for the right to conquer Ecuador, Colombia, and Guatemala, but Charles hesitated, probably because he was reluctant to introduce another forceful personality in the region, where the Crown's men jealously guarded their prerogatives. Instead, by virtue of the royal *asiento* (literally, assent) of April 1537, the king authorized de Soto to "conquer, pacify, and populate" the lands previously bestowed upon Narváez and Vazquez de Ayllón; it also sealed his appointment as governor of Cuba, a handy base from which to launch his expedition against Florida. The document stipulated that de Soto finance the undertaking himself and that salaries be drawn on future royal profits from the new province. In return, de Soto was allowed to import 150 slaves without paying duty on them and to stake out 12 square leagues of land for himself, so long as his acreage was not part of a seaport or city. He was also given the right to bestow encomiendas—grants of land and Indians—upon his colleagues. Charles reserved for the Crown half of any gold, silver, gems, and finery found, but de Soto could keep a sixth of any ransoms extorted—with the customary fifth for the Crown and the rest for the troops. The contract also banned lawyers from Florida and directed de Soto to

In the New World, Spanish noblemen were granted encomiendas—*grants of land and Indian slaves. Much theological debate was devoted to the question of whether Indians had a soul and could therefore rightfully be pressed into slavery, but by the time the issue was decided in favor of the Native Americans, hundreds of thousands of them had been killed.*

(continued on page 65)

The Shock of the New

De Soto at the Mississippi.

The only artistic portrayals of the New World that emerged from the de Soto expedition were literary ones. Readers of Biedma, Ranjel, Garcilaso de la Vega, and the Gentleman of Elvas could rely on only their own imaginations and the descriptive prose of these chroniclers to envision what the inhabitants of Florida looked like. One of the first Europeans to provide a visual record was the Englishman John White, who in 1585 sailed as a member of an expedition charged with reconnoitering the East Coast from the Chesapeake Bay to Florida. It may have been White's second journey to North America, but this time he left a permanent legacy of his visit to America: 75 watercolors documenting the richness and strangeness of the life Europeans were discovering across the Atlantic. This new world obviously exerted a powerful pull on White's imagination, for in 1587 he sailed west again, this time as commander of an expedition organized for the purpose of founding an English colony across the ocean. A settlement was established on Roanoke Island, off the coast of present-day North Carolina; Virginia Dare, the first English child born in America, was White's granddaughter. When the colony ran low on supplies, White sailed back to England; when he returned in 1590, he found the colony utterly abandoned, with no trace of the fate of its inhabitants.

A variety of native fishing methods, as well as several different types of fish, may be seen in this White watercolor. The Indian standing at the rear of the dugout canoe is raking the water to attract fish to the surface, whereupon he will capture them with the net he has kept close at hand. Above, Indians are spearing fish in shallower water; at left, an elaborate fencelike weir, or trap, holds fish for later collection.

White's map of the area visited by the 1585 expedition. Note that he has delineated as Virginia the entire region north of Florida and that he has incorrectly exaggerated the extent to which the East Coast falls away to the west.

A Flamingo.

60

On this page may be seen some of the flora and fauna of Florida as
White depicted it. Here is the leggy, large pink wading bird known as
the flamingo. Flamingos can be 3 to 5 feet in height and possess a broad
wingspan, long neck, webbed feet, and a distinctive downturned bill.

A jellyfish. White was somewhat confused about the powers of this marine invertebrate, which he claimed could fly. He noted at the top of the painting that some called the creatures "caravels," after the small Spanish vessels in which many of the great voyages of exploration to the New World were conducted.

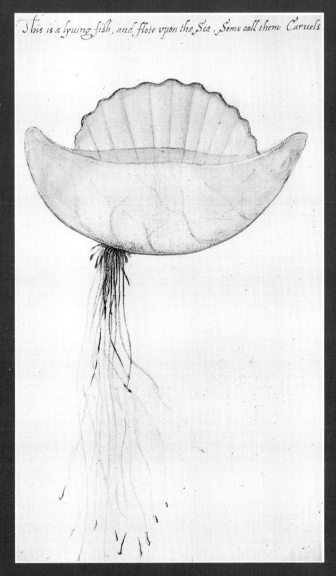

This is a lyuing fish, and flote vpon the Sea, Some call them Caruels

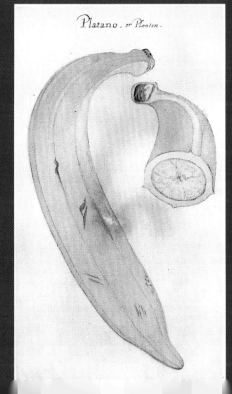

Platano. or Planten.

Horn plantain, a plant similar to the banana. It grows in tropical and semitropical climates.

An Indian couple share a bowl of hominy, a staple
food made by hulling and boiling the kernels of
Indian corn, then adding bits of fish and meat.

White's portrayal of an Indian woman of Florida. The woman is tattooed from her feet to her shoulders; in some Florida tribes both men and women decorated themselves in such fashion.

Of Florida.

Of Florida.

White's portrait of a Timucuan archer. The Florida Indians used much longer bows than did their counterparts farther up the Atlantic coast, and the English were amazed at the distance and accuracy they were able to obtain with these weapons.

65

An elaborate Indian fortification, sketched by White at a harbor on the Florida coast he called St. John's. White made sketches in the New World, then transformed them into detailed watercolors after returning to England. His work also appeared as line engravings by the popular Flemish artist Theodore de Bry.

(continued from page 56)

develop forts, harbors, and a hospital for the poor.

During the year that de Soto spent organizing his venture, Cabeza de Vaca resurfaced in Spain. His arrival only heightened expectations about the treasures to be found in Florida, and he agreed to accompany de Soto. The two had a falling-out, however, when de Soto balked at paying for a boat Cabeza de Vaca had requisitioned for the expedition. Cabeza de Vaca nevertheless encouraged his relatives, Baltasar de Gallegos and Cristobal de Espindola, to sign on with de Soto. This endorsement, coupled with the adelantado's reputation, spurred enlistments. Nobles sold their vineyards, olive groves, and wheat fields to buy a place on the roll, and tradesmen volunteered their skills.

This disparate assortment of would-be adventurers gathered in Seville, a bustling Moorish-looking city near the port of Sanlúcar, where de Soto's seven ships were taking on supplies. In early 1538, a company of Portuguese hidalgos captained by Andre de Vasconcelos joined the hopefuls. One of them, the Gentleman of Elvas, reported with a touch of nationalistic pride on de Soto's inspection:

> He commanded a muster to be made, to which the
> Portuguese turned out in polished armor, and the
> Castilians very showily, in silk over silk, pinked and
> slashed. As such luxury did not appear to him becoming
> on such occasion, he ordered a review to be called for the
> next day, when every man should appear with his arms; to
> which the Portuguese came as at first; and the Governor
> set them in order near the standard borne by his ensign.
> The greater number of the Castilians were in very sorry
> and rusty shirts of mail; all wore steel caps or helmets, but
> had very poor lances. Some of them sought to get among
> the Portuguese. Those that Soto liked and accepted of
> were passed, counted, and enlisted; six hundred men in all
> followed him to Florida.

Actually, according to historians who have sifted through the 4 accounts of the expedition and the official roster filed with the Council of the Indies, more than 700 people embarked at Sanlúcar. Besides the contingent of Portuguese, the adelantado enrolled only a few foreigners—a French priest, a Genoese engineer, a Sardinian, a Greek, and four men of color, perhaps former Moorish slaves. The majority of the Spaniards were young nobles who hailed from de Soto's home province of Badajoz. At least 6 tailors, 3 notaries, 2 shoemakers, a stocking maker, a trumpeter, a farrier (to shoe the horses), a caulker (to seal the boat seams), a sword cutler, 3 friars, 12 priests, and several pages and servants supplemented the ranks of soldiers and sailors. Like de Soto, several officers brought along their wives and families, who later debarked in Cuba, but three or four women accompanied the adventurers to the mainland.

To the blare of trumpets and the thunder of artillery, the fleet set sail in early April 1538. De Soto commanded the enormous (for its time) 800-ton flagship *San Cristobal* piloted by Alonso Martin. His most trusted officers took charge of the other vessels: Captain General Nuño de Tobar at the helm of the equally imposing *La Magadalena*, Master of Camp Luis Moscoso of the 500-ton *La Concepcion*, Andre de Vasconcelos of the *Buena Fortuna*, Diego Garcia of the *San Juan*, Infantry Captain Arias Tinoco of the *Santa Barbara*, and Alonso Romo de Cardenosa (Tinoco's brother) of the galleon *San Anton*. For mutual protection against pirates, another 20 vessels headed for New Spain traveled with them.

By Easter, the fleet had reached the Canary Islands off northwest Africa, where the governor, a relative of de Soto's wife, augmented its stores of bread, meat, and wine. To Doña Isabel, he also entrusted his daughter, Leonor de Bobadilla, as a maid-in-waiting, in the hope that she would find a good husband in Cuba—a kinsmanly act that would later undermine de Soto's chain of command. But for the moment, fair skies and favorable winds buoyed the voyagers.

The ships reached Cuba by the end of May. Always thorough, de Soto was in no hurry to reach Florida. To assure a suitable harbor for landing the expedition, he twice sent Juan de Añasco from Havana to reconnoiter the coast of the mainland. (On one trip Añasco returned with four Indian captives, whom de Soto assigned to learn Spanish for guide and interpreter duty.) Meanwhile, the governor cultivated the friendship of wealthy Vasco Porcallo de Figueroa and assembled provisions: 2,500 shoulders of bacon, 3,000 loads of cassava (a starchy root used as a bread substitute), and 5,000 bushels of maize, as well as iron, steel, forges, spades, ropes, baskets, breeches, sandals, knives, mirrors, and beads as gifts for cooperative natives, and iron collars as restraints for hostile ones. In addition to more than 230 cavalry horses and some greyhounds, de Soto had acquired a herd of tough, long-legged hogs as an ambulatory food supply. Although the adelantado's buying spree delighted the merchants of Cuba, the previous governor of the island appealed to the king to limit such expenditures in the future because greedy citizens were selling off vital seeds and livestock.

In addition to five of the large ships from Spain, de Soto loaded two caravels and two pinnaces for the short sprint to Florida. The year on Cuba may have benefited the men, helping them adjust to the New World's climate, but it did result in a few crew changes—most notably the demotion of Nuño de Tobar, who had impregnated Leonor de Bobadilla. Although the two married before the baby's birth, the adelantado, who believed that his wife's honor had been offended by the seduction of her comely young charge, replaced the capable, professional Tobar with the amateur Vasco Porcallo, who had donated so many supplies. But as the supremely well-equipped flotilla finally set sail from Havana in mid-May of 1539, the falling-out between Tobar and de Soto seemed unimportant amidst the high spirits and optimism that accompanied the departure.

The de Soto expedition embarks at Sanlúcar de Barrameda, Spain, in 1538. Among the more than 700 people of the expedition were tailors, notaries, shoemakers, a stocking maker, a farrier, a caulker, 3 friars, and 12 priests.

No Turning Back

Marking time, as always, with the church calendar, the Spaniards sighted land on Whitsunday, about a week after they left Cuba. Because Añasco had neglected to sound his chosen harbor, the enormous ships scraped the sand-and-mud bottom and almost ran aground as they approached the shore. Taking with him 300 soldiers, the adelantado rowed ashore and took possession of Florida in the name of King Charles I on or around May 30, 1539.

Traditionally, historians have placed the bay de Soto christened Espíritu Santo (Holy Spirit) at Tampa. The 1939 de Soto Commission, a fact-finding group appointed by the U.S. Congress in honor of the 400th anniversary of de Soto's landing, supported this conclusion with their voluminous report. Among the supporting evidence cited by the commission was the geographical descriptions in the four narratives of the journey and Tampa's location almost due north of Havana. Other researchers, however, have disagreed, pointing out that the four narratives are extremely vague and that compass navigation would aim the ships south and east of Tampa. While Añasco reportedly found a port 75 to 80 leagues from Havana, it is not clear whether he was measuring by land leagues (2.6 miles) or nautical leagues (3.2 miles). In *De Soto Didn't Land at Tampa*, Floridian Rolfe F. Schell makes a convincing case for landfall in the Charlotte Harbor area, the location favored by many modern scholars. The debate

The Spaniards were amazed by the lush flora and unusual fauna they encountered in the swamplands of Florida, but they proved unable to live off the land. As they plodded through the mire, the Spaniards sustained themselves on whatever stores they could appropriate from Indian villages.

illustrates the many difficulties historians can have in trying to paint a coherent picture of the past.

While the remaining men, women, pigs, dogs, and horses came ashore, Vasco Porcallo and a scouting party startled six Indians in the woods, two of whom died resisting capture as the others fled. The army then marched inland to the village of Ucita, which they discovered to be abandoned. De Soto, Porcallo, and Moscoso occupied the chief's house, which was built on a mound by the beach. "At the other end of the town," wrote Elvas, "was a temple, on the top of which perched a wood fowl with gilded eyes, and within were found some pearls of small value, injured by fire." The soldiers tore down the temple and a few huts before building their own temporary cabins.

Two of the Indian interpreters seized by Añasco escaped, so de Soto, who, like most prudent commanders, relied on local intelligence, sent out his captains to round up natives. When a phalanx of 40 horsemen and 80 footsoldiers encountered some Indians in an open field, they charged—against the orders of their commander, Baltasar de Gallegos. As the Inca remarked, "Who can do anything with raw recruits when they are disordered?" According to Garcilaso, hotheaded lancers were trying to skewer the Indians when one of the tanned and tattooed men cried "Xivilla, Xivilla," meaning Seville. Since the Spaniards did not understand, the soon-to-be victim made a sign of the cross with his hand and the bow. He was not a Native American but a survivor from the shore party that had tried to save Narváez. His name was Juan Ortiz.

The Spanish were fascinated by Ortiz's story. He and three other Spaniards had fallen into the hands of Hirrihigua, who repaid them for the mutilation and death of his mother by barbecuing them over coals on a wooden grill. The shrieks of young Ortiz nonetheless touched the chief's wife and daughters, who cajoled Hirrihigua into sparing the teenager—"not, however, before he was halfbaked and blisters that looked like halves of oranges had

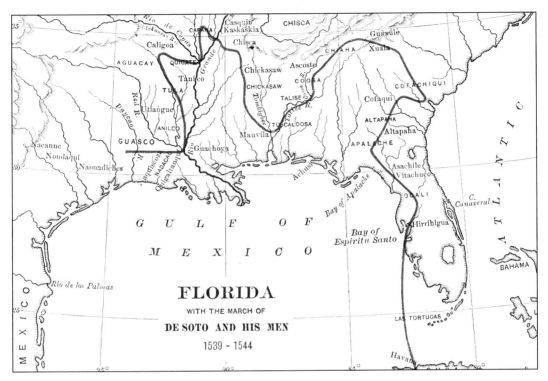

FLORIDA

WITH THE MARCH OF

DE SOTO AND HIS MEN

1539 - 1544

formed on one of his sides," reported Garcilaso. Ortiz's scars attested to his suffering. To the Spaniards, his nakedness was nearly as appalling, and they hustled him into clothes.

Although the Indian women salved the boy's sores with herb juice, the chief continued to torment him, assigning him to guard an above-ground cemetery. One night, as the exhausted Ortiz snoozed, a wolf (or possibly a panther; the Inca called the beast a "lion") seized a child's corpse. The boy stalked the beast into the forest and killed it with a spear. His bravery impressed the chief, but, alas, the reprieve did not last long. As the Inca explained, each time Hirrihigua "attempted to blow his nose and failed to find it, the Devil seized him with the thought of avenging himself on Juan Ortiz."

Fearing for the boy's safety, Hirrihigua's daughter directed him to a neighboring village. There, the benevolent

This map follows the trail of the de Soto expedition from its landing near Tampa Bay (Bay of Espíritu Santo) through the present-day states of Georgia, South Carolina, Alabama, Mississippi, Arkansas, and Louisiana.

Juan Ortiz, a survivor of the shore party that tried to save Narváez, was captured by Hirrihigua and made to pay for Narváez's transgressions. Here, Hirrihigua (the artist has portrayed him with his nose intact) lectures Ortiz on the punishment that is in store for him.

chief Mocozo welcomed him as one of the tribe. When de Soto heard of Mocozo's kindness, he conveyed gifts and gratitude to the chief, who responded with equal, albeit nervous, goodwill.

Yet other Indians in the area did not trust the invaders and continued to evade them. Certain that the riches of the empire lay inland, as they had in Mexico and Peru, de Soto kept his scouts combing the territory for informants. The results were discouraging. When sparring with natives, harquebusiers could load and fire only one gunshot for every three deadly arrows sent zinging their way. For all of their renowned military innovation, the Spaniards did not have a strategy for swamp warfare. Vasco Porcallo, who had planned to trap slaves for his plantation and instead found himself wallowing in slime, decided to quit. De Soto sent all but three ships with him back to Cuba to secure more supplies, but perhaps also to prevent other disgruntled soldiers from deserting.

In mid-July, the adelantado stationed Pedro Calderon and a well-provisioned garrison of about 100 men on the coast and advanced west and then north to Paracoxi, where yet another chief had gone into hiding. Messengers, however, relayed communications to the effect that in the province of Cale grain abounded and warriors wore helmets of gold. But to get there, the Spanish soon found out, they first had to cross a vast swamp. Next, at a large river, the Genoese engineer supervised the construction of a wooden bridge for the men, who drew the horses across with ropes. The hardy hogs swam.

Although it was tough terrain for men in full suits of armor, the Florida landscape supported lots of wildlife—panthers, bears, deer, rabbits, partridges, ducks, pigeons, thrushes, sparrows, and birds of prey, according to Elvas. Insects buzzed among the blooming flowers; pears, plums, and grapes grew wild. But a column as large as de Soto's scared away the animals (the Spaniards were not great hunters, anyway) and quickly consumed everything in its path. In small, deserted villages, the Spaniards simply helped themselves to all available foodstuffs. Whenever possible, de Soto tried to bargain with the Indians, but he had difficulty getting them to negotiate, probably because the reputation of the Spanish for cruelty had preceded them. According to the Inca, the chief of the province of Acuera, near present-day Orlando, ordered his underlings to behead any of the "professional vagabonds" they could ambush. De Soto in turn amputated the hands and noses of captive tribesmen as a message to defiant caciques. (Back in lawless 15th-century Castile, the Santa Hermandad, a national police force, had punished highwaymen with the loss of a limb for a crime. Although the need for vigilantes had waned in Spain, de Soto may have derived his tactics from this vestige of the justice of the Middle Ages.) Between settlements, as stores ran low, the soldiers, like the hogs, foraged for unripe maize and palmetto cabbages.

Finally, in Cale (in the region of present-day Ocala), the Spanish found enough maize, beans, and "small dogs" (probably opossum) to gorge themselves on, and de Soto ordered his men to load enough grain for three months. Angry at being robbed of their harvest, the Indians (probably the agricultural Ais) killed three of the invaders. As he frequently did, de Soto then divided his army, riding ahead with scouts and leaving Master of Camp Moscoso in charge of the encampment.

The Indians of Florida had developed many ingenious methods that allowed them to thrive within their environment. This late-16th-century woodcut shows Indian braves disguised in deerskin as they lay in wait for unsuspecting bucks at a stream.

At Caliquen in mid-August, de Soto's party took about 20 prisoners, including the daughter of a chief. From them the Spaniards learned of Apalache and Narváez's travails there. "Every mind was depressed at this information," wrote Elvas, "and all counselled the Governor to go back to the port, that they might not be lost, as Narváez had been, and to leave the land of Florida." But de Soto reckoned himself a more astute explorer than Narváez and sent orders back to Moscoso directing him to come forward. Then, with the chief, his daughter, and a high-ranking guide as hostages, the Spaniards marched north. Ahead lay Napituca.

After the battle of the lakes and the subsequent rebellion of the captives, the nervous Spaniards took to chaining their Indian slaves with iron neck collars. According to Elvas:

> Sometimes it happened that, going with them for wood or maize, they would kill the Christian, and flee, with the chain on, which others would file at night with a splinter of stone, in the place of iron, at which work, when

De Bry engraved this gruesome scene of de Soto meting out justice to the native inhabitants of the New World, which illustrated a 17th-century edition of Las Casas's Brief Account of the Destruction of the Indies.

caught, they were punished, as a warning to others. . . .
The women and youths, when removed a hundred leagues
from their country, no longer cared, and were taken along
loose, doing the work, and in a very little time learning
the Spanish language.

Unfettered natives, however, continued to skirmish with
the Spaniards. The army trudged on, building bridges over
the Suwannee and Aucilla rivers, following Indian trails
out of Timucua country to Apalache. In early October,
it reached the main town of the province, which had been
abandoned but was still well stocked with corn, pumpkin,
maize, and squash. Deer and fish were plentiful. Behind
wooden fortifications, the Spaniards and their prisoners
settled in for the winter.

As always, de Soto dispatched his captains to sketch the
lay of the land. Juan de Añasco's company searched for
the sea—with much hardship, the Inca reported, because
an Indian deliberately led them astray. After killing him
and seizing new guides (some of whom spoke a little Spanish), they discovered the bay where Narváez had bivouacked: There remained the charcoal of his forge,
wooden mangers, and the skulls of horses. The Spaniards
peered into the hollows of nearby trees, but Narváez had
not left any messages. (De Soto often did, but for his own
soldiers, not future explorers.)

When Añasco informed de Soto that a good harbor lay
nearby, the adelantado decided to regroup his forces, despite the dangers inherent in doing so. In order to fetch
the garrison and the 2 ships at the Bay of the Holy Spirit,
30 cavaliers would have to retrace the entire journey—not
once, but twice. De Soto tapped the redoubtable Añasco
to lead the daring mission.

Traveling fast and circumventing towns at night, the 30
lancers crossed icy rivers and dodged hostile Indians all
the way back to the territory of kindly Mocozo. There,
they reunited with Calderon, whose force was in good
shape except for the loss of a few troublemakers who had

*The de Soto expedition on bivouac
in a lush Florida forest, in a scene
illustrating the contrast between
Christian belief and the cruel
practices of the conquistadores.
At right center, priests march with
soldiers under the cross while
at lower right Indians in chains
are guarded by dogs.*

been killed by Indians they had provoked. One of Calderon's pages, Diego Muñoz, had also been captured. The
captains nonetheless rewarded Mocozo with mounds of
cassava, cloaks, shoes, helmets, cables—all the supplies
the two brigantines could not hold. On the adelantado's
orders, Gomez Arias sailed the remaining caravel to Havana to deliver greetings to Doña Isabel and to inform the
citizens of Cuba "of the fine qualities which they had seen
in the land of Florida."

Añasco and the brigantines rendezvoused with de Soto's
lookouts in Apalache at the end of November; a month
later, the landsmen arrived, looking frayed and hungry.
"The Governor welcomed his captain and soldiers as
would a loving father," the Inca noted, "joyfully embrac-
ing and questioning each of them individually as to how
he felt and how he had withstood the journey." Two decades in the military had honed de Soto's talent for leadership: When greed could no longer sustain the Spaniards,
loyalty would.

De Soto sent Infantry captain Francisco Maldonado in
the brigantines to scout the coast. Meanwhile, a young
Indian from Napituca, whom the Spaniards had nicknamed Perico, entertained his captors with a story about
a marvelous land located near the rising sun where a
woman ruler was paid tribute by many powerful chiefs.
During the long winter nights, Perico described the yield
from the gold mines there so convincingly that his eager
listeners felt sure that this kingdom would outshine Mexico
and Peru in riches. Maldonado returned with more good
news, about a sheltered port worthy of a colony about 60
leagues west of Apalache, at Achusi, today's Pensacola.
As he prepared to march east, de Soto dispatched Maldonado and the ships back to Cuba, where they were to
resupply. A rendezvous was planned at Achusi for the
following summer.

The army departed in March 1540. Because so many
of the naked and chained Indian porters had died during

the winter, the troops were now forced to carry their own rations. Two days out, the march stalled at the wide Capacheguy River. The Spanish were able to ford it only by improvising a rope-and-cable system that prevented their barge and horses from being washed downstream by the powerful current.

To the Spaniards, the villages of different tribes in Florida had looked mostly alike, but as they passed into present-day Georgia, they noticed a change. Grass roofs gave way to cane ones, and the explorers admired the cleanliness of the cabins. According to Elvas, these Indians, the Creeks, owned two houses each, a winter one plastered with clay and "heated like an oven" by a fire, and a summer one, located near a kitchen where cornbread was baked. The Indian men wore colorful, dyed deerskins; the women, skirts of bark or nettle grass. The Creeks were also more cooperative than the Timucuan had been in supplying de Soto with turkeys, partridges, maize, and guides.

But beyond the luxurious province of Patofa, conditions

Before marching off to war, a Florida Indian chief observes the contortions of a tribal wise man, who is seeking auspicious omens for the upcoming battle. The opposition of the Indians would dog de Soto for the rest of his journey, particularly once word of his atrocities spread from village to village.

Indian women beg assistance from the chief as the bodies of their dead husbands are carried off by attendants. The European presence in the New World (the Spanish were followed by the English, the Dutch, and the French) resulted not only in the death of hundreds of thousands of Indians but also in the destruction of entire cultures.

worsened. Some of the few surviving Indian porters disappeared into the pine forests, and in this uninhabited region, the soldiers could not easily replenish their stores. De Soto blamed Perico, who had been acting as lead guide, for underestimating the distance to the treasure kingdom, and the Indian youth finally admitted that he was lost. If he had not been the only Indian Juan Ortiz could understand, wrote Elvas, the furious adelantado would have hurled him to the greyhounds. Finally, de Soto sent the Indian servants home, agreed to butcher some of the herd of hogs, and issued half a pound of pork for each man each day. His scouts seized 4 Indians, one of whom, under threat of burning, pointed the army toward their destination of Cofitachequi, about 25 miles below present-day Augusta.

The cacica Perico had spoken about was awaiting the Spaniards at the Savannah River. After stepping from her canopied canoe, she chatted with de Soto—"quite graceful and at her ease," wrote Ranjel. Her stately conduct inspired the Spanish, who were often less than chivalrous in their behavior toward Indian women, to dub her La Señora de (the Lady of) Cofitachequi.

To help prevent confrontation, the cacica had sent half of the people of her town away so that she could accommodate the strangers. She was also quick to offer them grain and requested in return only that they leave half of the stockpile for her people. In a gesture of friendship, La Señora presented the adelantado with her own necklace, "a large strand of pearls as thick as hazelnuts which encircled her neck three times and fell to her thighs," according to the Inca. De Soto, in turn, slipped an elegant gold-and-ruby ring off his finger and handed it to her. La Señora's people loaned the soldiers canoes to cross the river and gave them deerskins and shawls of feather or bark, but the Spaniards indicated by pointing at their rings that what they truly desired was gold, silver, and gems.

The Native Americans proffered what they had—copper and slabs of shiny iron pyrite. La Señora directed de Soto to sepulchers where, among the decaying corpses of Indian nobles, he and his men found more than 350 pounds of carved freshwater pearls, somewhat discolored by burial and fire (part of the Creek technique for removing them from oyster shells). Rather than encumber the expedition, de Soto planned to haul a mere 50 pounds of the gems to Havana as a sample of Florida's riches, but according to the Inca, de Soto bowed to the wishes of his men and issued 2 handfuls to everyone so that they could make rosaries.

In Cofitachequi, the Spaniards also unearthed a dagger and some false pearls, which they figured to be vestiges of the Vazquez de Ayllón expedition, since scouts had located a sea harbor within two days' travel. Despite this sad reminder and the absence of precious metals, many of the explorers wished to found a settlement there. The countryside—open forests of walnut and mulberry trees, fertile stream-fed fields—charmed the Spaniards. Once in encomiendas, the Indians would deliver to their masters undamaged pearls, suitable for shipping back to the motherland from the port, which would become a convenient stopping place for cargo fleets from New Spain.

De Soto squelched this daydreaming. He argued that the land could not support the troops for more than a month, that Maldonado was expecting them back at Achusi, that they could always fall back on this place if they found nothing better. He pressed the natives for news of richer country; they mentioned a place called Coca, located more than 150 miles west on the Coosa River in Alabama. As always, de Soto, "being an inflexible man," Elvas said, "who, although he liked to know what the others all thought and had to say, after he once said a thing he did not like to be opposed," prevailed over the wishes of his men.

Artfully camouflaged in the dark forest surrounding them, Indians prepare to attack the Spaniards. The Native Americans would often track their enemy for miles until the time was right for their assault.

The Death
of a Dream

Despite the cacica's generous diplomacy, the Spaniards were unable to contain themselves, and their "outrages"— Elvas's word for theft and rape—led La Señora to refuse her parting guests the services of guides or porters. This sudden obstinacy did not much trouble de Soto, who simply arrested and kidnapped her. Using native trails, the expedition marched north across the piedmont of South Carolina, through very poor country where naked Indians, probably Cheraw, dug for herbs. In the vicinity of Xuala, a village at the foot of the Blue Ridge Mountains, La Señora and several of her servants escaped, taking with them a *pateca* (a cane box) of pristine pearls. Although Ranjel reported that evidence of gold was found in the region, the hungry Spaniards pressed on. Three slaves (a black, a Cuban Indian, and a Berber) and two soldiers deserted, however, in order to pursue Indian women.

The explorers hiked over the ridge into Cherokee territory, to the town of Guasili, where cooperative Indians fed them dogs, corn, and mulberries and shouldered some of the loads. With their help, de Soto's party trekked a difficult path along the gorge of the Hiwassee River below present-day Murphy, North Carolina, and exited the highlands at the Tennessee River. Downstream, they passed the future site of the city of Chattanooga and reached the village of Chiaha on Burns Island. In three weeks, the army—the first Europeans to cross the Appalachian

La Señora de Cofitachequi shows de Soto her rich supply of pearls and precious stones. Eager to save her people, La Señora gave the Spaniards food and lodging and bestowed gifts of pearls upon them.

Mountains—had traveled over 150 miles. It would not be until well into the next century that European explorers—Frenchmen, this time—would again delve into the interior of the Southeast.

At Chiaha, the Spaniards and their horses regained their strength. The local chief shared maize, bear fat, walnut oil, and honey with his visitors, and together the Indians and the strangers swam and fished. But once again the Spaniards abused native hospitality when de Soto requested 30 female slaves for his sex-starved officers. That night, the men of Chiaha smuggled their women and children out of town, and the chief surrendered soon afterward. With him as a guide, de Soto, 30 cavaliers, and a battalion of infantry scoured the area, chopping down the fields of maize outside fenced villages. Only when the adelantado promised to forget about the women did the families return, and 500 Indians were made to serve as porters for the next leg of the journey.

De Soto reached Cosa, near present-day Childersburg, Alabama, in early July. There, the cacique, dressed in a cloak of marten skins and a feathered crown, greeted the

The desire for gold was the single greatest factor that motivated the Spanish in their conquest of the Americas. This 16th-century engraving purports to show the techniques used by Indians in the Appalachian Mountains to gather gold from streams.

Spaniards from a litter carried on the shoulders of his councilmen. The expedition rested for nearly a month in this rich Creek Indian province, then continued into Choctaw country. As usual, de Soto had his men seize the chief to ensure the compliance of his subjects. Although the cacique was later released, Ranjel noted that he departed from the Spanish expedition "in tears because the governor would not give up his sister."

Down the Alabama River, near where it joins the Tombigbee, the powerful chief Tascaluza sent messengers, his son among them, to bid the strangers welcome. Seated on a platform on a mound in his village, surrounded by his nobles (one of whom held a parasol to shade Tascaluza from the sun), the tall and sober chief impressed the Spaniards with his kingly indifference to their military parade. He spoke only to de Soto, who, despite a flowery show of friendship during two days in town, put the chief under guard. In answer to the Spaniards' demands for more carriers, Tascaluza promised them 100 women when the expedition reached the town of Mauvilla, north of today's Mobile.

De Soto's scouts warned him that the Mauvillans appeared to be preparing for battle, as they were busy laying in provisions and bolstering the palisade—a fence of thick wooden stakes bound by cane and plastered with mud and straw—yet the chief's messengers greeted the Spanish with bread made from chestnuts. This was enough for de Soto to disregard the advice of his scouts and Moscoso, who warned him to be wary of a trap. Ever confident, de Soto decided to lead a vanguard into town, assuming that a show of bravery on the part of the conquistadores would be sufficient to cow the natives.

On the morning of October 18, 1540, native flute players escorted the adelantado's party to the main piazza of Mauvilla. During the native dances, Tascaluza excused himself to talk with the resident chief. When called back by de Soto, Tascaluza replied with defiance, which

De Soto and his men cross the Tombigbee River, in present-day Alabama, in the fall of 1540. For the next two years Indian ambushes, disease, and a breakdown in discipline hampered the expedition.

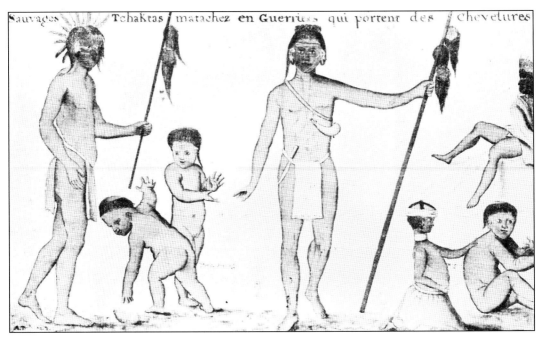

Sauvages   Tchaktas matachez en Guerre qui portent des   Chevelures

A French traveler in Louisiana in the 1730s drew this rather crude sketch of Choctaw warriors brandishing spears decorated with the scalps of their enemies. De Soto and his men had ample opportunity to experience the martial prowess of the Choctaw at the village of Mauvilla.

prompted Baltasar de Gallegos to strike an Indian. Suddenly, thousands of Indians poured out of their houses, yelling and firing arrows. With the Indians in hot pursuit, most of the Spaniards scrambled out the gate.

The cavalry tried to mount their horses, or at least cut their halters, but the Indians grabbed some of the animals, along with the packs and baskets the carriers had propped up against the palisade. On the plain outside of town, de Soto called for a mount and lanced a few of the pursuers. The rest regrouped in their walled village, shooting arrows into the field, waving the Spaniards' belongings to the beat of drums.

As reinforcements arrived, de Soto organized an assault. He ordered 60 of the best-armed horsemen to dismount. Divided into four squadrons, they were to attack the fortress from four sides. In each squadron, one soldier carried a brand with which to set fire to the houses, thereby driving the Indians onto the plain, where the surrounding cavalry could mow them down as the infantry charged in through the gate. The plan worked, but the Indians resisted fiercely, even hanging or immolating themselves rather than bowing to the invaders. De Soto spearheaded the action, galloping into the main plaza with Nuño de Tobar at his side. However, as he stood in his stirrups to deliver one fatal puncture, an Indian aimed an arrow at a gap in his armor and struck him in the left buttock, according to the Inca. For the next five hours of furious fighting, and no doubt for some time afterward, the fearsome adelantado could not sit back in his saddle.

"The struggle lasted so long that many Christians, weary and very thirsty, went to drink at a pond near by, tinged with the blood of the killed, and returned to combat," Elvas witnessed. By the end of the day, at least 2,500 Indians had died. Although the Spaniards had prevailed, they lost 22 men according to Ranjel, including de Soto's nephew and brother-in-law; 150 to 250 more had sustained injuries from arrows; and over 80 horses were hurt or dead. The fire had also consumed most of their possessions—clothes, food, pearls, medicine. Biedma said the company dressed their wounds with the fat of dead Indians.

Including the casualties from this battle, 102 Spaniards had died since setting foot on the mainland. As the army

The Spaniards enter Mauvilla in October 1540. De Soto confidently advanced on the town even after his scouts warned him that its chief, Tascaluza, was preparing an ambush for him there.

De Soto meets with chief Tascaluza in the central plaza of Mauvilla. Native musicians escorted de Soto and his advance guard to the meeting, lending the occasion a festive air, but if the Spaniards had been more observant they might have noticed Indian archers strategically placed for an attack.

recuperated near Mauvilla, de Soto received confirmation through Indian captives that Maldonado's ships were anchored in Achusi, less than 30 leagues (about 80 miles) distant. De Soto had been planning to ship some of the pearls of Cofitachequi back to Havana, but they now lay scorched in the ashes of Mauvilla. The adelantado was also troubled by a rumor that his treasurer, Juan Gaytan, who had long spoken of his desire to bail out and sail back to civilization, was hatching a mutiny plot among the officers. But even though ships were waiting to carry himself and all of his homesick, hungry, and rebellious men back to Cuba, de Soto decided to keep Maldonado waiting. He knew that if the explorers returned home in this miserable condition—battered, emaciated, wounded, without any treasure—his reputation would suffer, and he would never be able to muster a second expedition to Florida. Leaving Maldonado to fend for himself, de Soto told his men that they needed to find a base for the winter, and they set off north, away from the coast.

In November 1540, after crossing the Black Warrior and Tombigbee rivers, the explorers reached the Chickasaw Indian territory of northeastern Mississippi. Cold rain chilled the adventurers; on Christmas it turned to snow. They quartered in an abandoned town, adding new huts built of wood and straw to the 200 already there. Perhaps feeling more vulnerable than when he had landed, de Soto tried to woo the cooperation of the displaced cacique and his chiefs by feasting them with pork, but the Indians developed such a taste for the meat that they started poaching pigs at night. When the Spaniards finally apprehended three swine stealers, de Soto ordered two executed and the third sent back to his tribe—minus his hands. When four Spaniards were caught pilfering from a cacique, de Soto sentenced two of them to beheading in order to appease the angry victims, but Juan Ortiz intentionally mistranslated the message of some Indian emissaries to fool de Soto into sparing them. Discipline, always fragile, was breaking down.

In March of the new year 1541, the adelantado demanded 200 porters from the cacique. Although the chief agreed, de Soto was suspicious. According to Ranjel, he cautioned Moscoso to post an extra-attentive watch and ordered his men to sleep fully armed, with their horses saddled. Yet two of the three horsemen the field marshal assigned to sentry duty had a history of incompetence. In the wee hours of the morning, the Chickasaw, later renowned among European colonists for their savvy in warfare, silently converged on the Spaniards' camp, then attacked, whooping and sounding noisemakers as they fired flaming arrows into the village. The groggy Spaniards, who had not prepared for battle, ran in all directions and were easy targets in the light of the spreading bonfire.

Only a few soldiers and de Soto, who according to the Inca always slept in his doublet and breeches, were able to mount and counterattack. Most of the men, however, could not find their weapons or horses in the confusion.

All of the chroniclers agree that the Indians would have been able to massacre the invaders had not panicked horses broken their halters and stampeded out of town, creating the false impression that the cavalry was charging.

The Indians withdrew, minus one warrior killed by de Soto. The Spaniards, on the other hand, suffered terrible losses: about a dozen dead, including one woman, Francisca de Hinestrosa, an officer's wife who was burned alive; more than 50 horses torched; and, between Mauvilla and this battle, at least three quarters of the hogs reduced to ashes. Nothing remained of the town and the few packs they had salvaged from Mauvilla.

After regrouping in another village a league away, the approximately 450 remaining explorers braced for another attack. Hastily, they set up a forge, made bellows out of bearskins, and repaired whatever weapons and saddles they had salvaged. Inexplicably, the Indians did not launch a follow-up attack for more than a week, during which time the Spaniards fashioned new lances out of ash trees. At night, the half-naked, half-frozen explorers covered themselves in grass mats and tried to sleep by large fires, which probably unnerved the skittish horses. Because of the sentries' failure, de Soto sacked Moscoso in favor of Baltasar de Gallegos, who made sure his watch sounded the alarm when the Chickasaw tried another pre-dawn assault. This time, the Spaniards squared off with the Indians on open ground and routed them.

After another month of regrouping, in April 1541, de Soto's army headed west from the Yazoo Delta region toward the Mississippi River. On a raid for grain, Juan de Añasco's scouting party came upon a fortified roadblock where natives in striped war paint lay in wait. The captain advised the adelantado to avoid an encounter, but de Soto worried that unless the Spaniards made a show of force, the Indians would become that much more belligerent later on. He organized an offensive, and although the Indians eventually retreated, they killed 15 Spaniards in the course of the fighting. His men blamed de Soto for provoking the confrontation and then executing the attack poorly. Its progress hampered by the large amounts of injured and wounded, including two badly burned soldiers who were carried on stretchers by Indian slaves, the ragged army moved slowly onward.

By this point, the expedition had no fixed destination; warfare and marauding had become ends in themselves. Near the village of Quizquiz, the rapacious Spaniards seized more than 300 women for the purpose of satisfying their unholy desires. That day or the next, around the 8th of May, the Spaniards came upon the Mississippi, which they named the Rio Grande (Great River). "Many of the conquerors said this river was larger than the Danube," Ranjel reported, but they had no inkling of the actual magnitude of this winding inland waterway, the third longest in the world after the Nile and the Amazon. Despite Pineda's exploration around the river's mouth in 1519 and Narváez's visit in 1528, history texts have traditionally credited de Soto with the first European sighting of the Father of Waters.

Near the steep riverbank, the Spaniards cut down trees and built four piraguas, or rafts, as ferries with which to cross the turbid spring floodwaters. Every afternoon, Indians paddled by in canoes to launch a barrage of arrows, but from such a distance they fell short of the trenches the invaders had dug. After four weeks, the frail rafts were ready. Although the swift current carried them downstream, the men, pigs, and horses crossed without incident. (The 1939 de Soto Commission placed the crossing in the vicinity of Sunflower Landing, Mississippi, but it should always be remembered that much about the de Soto expedition is still the subject of intense historical debate. Some historians even believe that recently unearthed archaeological evidence threatens to prove incorrect the entire course traditionally credited to the de Soto expedition.)

At Mauvilla, the Indians, as usual, suffered more casualties than the Spanish. Many of the Indians took their own life rather than be taken prisoner by the ruthless explorers. But the Spanish did not escape unscathed, and after Mauvilla, de Soto had to rest his troops for a month so that they could nurse their wounds.

On the Arkansas side of the river, the explorers admired the fortified Indian towns they came upon. At Casqui, Ranjel noted that "many skulls of bulls [most likely buffalo heads], very fierce" hung above a large ceremonial building. Deer, panthers, and bearskins obtained at the village of Pacaha were used by the Spanish to refurbish their tattered wardrobe, and the soldiers fashioned armor for their horses from Indian shields made of cowhide. In no particular hurry to be anyplace, the strangers sojourned in the Pacaha region (de Soto made peace between two neighboring chiefs) while scouts canvassed the countryside. On one such mission north, Biedma's party interviewed a band of nomadic Indians who lived in tipis, but they were able to learn nothing of treasure.

In August, de Soto's troops began meandering west. Outside of Quiguate, a large town probably located on the St. Francis River, they were forced to wade through ponds. According to Elvas, the chains of the Indian captives rat-

The Spaniards try to mount a counterattack against the fleeing Chickasaw. The Indians lost only one warrior in the surprise attack, whereas the Spanish suffered the loss of 12 members of their party, 50 horses, and most of their herd of voracious hogs. If panic-stricken horses had not started to stampede, the Spaniards' losses would have been far worse.

tled through the mud, "by which the fish, becoming stupe-
fied, would swim to the surface," where the Spaniards
clubbed them. At today's Pine Bluff, they discovered the
Arkansas River and shadowed its fertile banks south to the
town of Coligua (probably present-day Little Rock). Without salt, the Spanish had suffered greatly in the summer
heat, but at Coligua they learned an Indian technique for
separating it from the sand of the brackish river. "There
were some who felt such a craving for it that on finding
it plentiful, they ate it in mouthfuls and alone as if it were
sugar," the Inca said.

Beyond the Province of Salt, in the Ouachita Mountain
foothills, the Caddo Indians of Tula surprised the invaders
with the ferocity of their resistance. They defended their
village from the rooftops using lances with fire-hardened
tips, according to Ranjel, who called them the "best fighting people the Christians met with." About 40 Caddos
died; they injured 7 or 8 Spaniards.

Reports of a "great water" now enticed de Soto to the
southeast, to Utiangue, near present-day Camden, Arkansas, where the army bivouacked for the winter. In the
spring, the adelantado planned to locate the sea, build two
brigantines, and send them to Cuba for reinforcements.
Despite severe cold and heavy snow, the soldiers weathered
the next four months in relative comfort. They fenced in
the town, helped themselves to stores of maize, beans,
walnuts, and firewood, learned from the Indians how to
snare rabbits in a trap, and dispatched the slaves to hunt
deer. Although the Mauvilla fire had destroyed their playing cards, gambling remained a popular pastime with the
soldiers, who fashioned new decks out of parchment.

Yet by the springtime, at the end of his third year on
the mainland, even de Soto could muster little energy or
enthusiasm for further exploration and plunder. According
to Elvas, he had only 300 "efficient men" and 40 horses,
mostly lame, who could not canter over rough terrain
because the farrier had no iron with which to make them

shoes. During the winter, Juan Ortiz had died. His Timucua training had helped the group negotiate with (or threaten) all the Muskogean-language peoples, but his replacement, a captive from Cofitachequi, could not really understand the local Indians, the Choctaw. Obtaining directions sometimes took a whole day, and even then, the Spaniards frequently got lost. The thickly forested Ozark plateau presented an even greater obstacle to further westward advance.

So in March 1542, de Soto backtracked southeast, toward the big river. With more men, perhaps, the expedition could return to Georgia and start a settlement. From Caddo country, the Spaniards entered the provinces of the Ais and Asinai Indians of central Louisiana. After tramping through driving snow and wading across treacherous swamps, the Spaniards reached the swollen Ouachita River, where one man drowned in crossing. Despite frequent skirmishes with Indians, they made it through a corn-rich, well-populated area to Guachoya, near the Mississippi River and today's town of Ferriday, where a friendly chief gave them fish to eat and animal skins for clothing.

Ill with fever, de Soto suspected that the Guachoya wanted to use the strangers to gain an advantage over their enemies, a desire that he was willing to accommodate. He treated Quigaltam, the visiting leader of Guachoya's cross-river neighbor, to his usual insolent spiel demanding immediate surrender, but the unimpressed Indian defiantly answered that he would believe de Soto was the child of the sun when he dried up the river; otherwise, the cacique would not stir. Too weak to cross the river to punish such boldness, de Soto sent 15 cavalry under Tobar and a company of infantry under Juan de Guzman to attack an unsuspecting village in order to instill fear in all the Indians of the area. The squad carried out its orders with a vengeance, massacring more than 100 men and imprisoning about 80 women and children. The Guachoya did indeed profit from the Spaniards: In the wake of the slaughter, they plundered the houses of their traditional enemy.

This butchery proved insufficient to invigorate the ailing adelantado, who had reasons besides his physical woes for despair. The expedition that he had launched with such hopes had descended into folly, a marathon walkabout of pillage, rape, and killing. For all their savagery, the Spaniards had not succeeded in pacifying a single region for colonization, and they had found no gold or silver; the pearls of Cofitachequi were now nothing but a distant memory. The sea no longer could be reached with a short march, for Juan de Añasco's scouting forays down the river had revealed only dense shrubs, canebrakes, and bogs. Even if the expedition succeeded in reaching the coast and sailing, de Soto did not anticipate a happy homecoming in either Mexico, Havana, or Seville. In New Spain, rival conquistadores would try to thwart his attempt to equip another expedition. Charles I might easily revoke de Soto's one paid post, as the governor of Cuba; the emperor, like the public, preferred to back winners. Contemporaries blamed de Soto's feverish decline on everything from shame to Indians to "the bloody flux," but certainly disappointment aggravated what was probably malaria or typhoid. Solicitous of their own well-being, fearful lest they, too, like so many of their erstwhile companions, should perish in the seemingly endless wilderness, the adelantado's soldiers shunned his sickbed, "each one himself having need of sympathy," Elvas noted.

Recognizing that his end was near, de Soto assembled his officers. Before them he confessed his sins to God and thanked the army for its perseverance and loyalty, then named the popular Luis Moscoso as his successor. On May 21, 1542, "the magnanimous, the virtuous, the intrepid Captain, Don Hernando de Soto" died at the age of 42. "He was advanced by fortune, in the way she is wont to lead others, that he might fall the greater depth," Elvas wrote.

De Soto gazes out over the wide Mississippi River, which he reached in May 1541. The expedition crossed the Father of Waters without incident and then meandered, looting and killing, seemingly with no fixed objective in mind.

The Empty-Handed Return

The grieving and frightened Spaniards buried de Soto's body that night in town without a marker, in order to hide the loss of their feared leader from the Indians. When asked what had happened to the ill commander, Moscoso replied that the immortal de Soto had climbed into the sky for a prolonged, but not unusual, visit. As Elvas recorded, this poppycock did not deceive anyone; one chief, in fact, offered to sacrifice two of his braves so that they could accompany the dead leader to heaven. Afraid that the Indians would discover the grave, the Spaniards dug up the corpse after dark, weighted down the body, and sank it in the middle of the Mississippi.

In his 1539 will executed back in Cuba, de Soto acknowledged that half of his estate belonged to his partner Hernan Ponce (who had not accompanied him on the expedition); the rest he willed to his wife, with special provisions for his illegitimate children, his servants, and any poor orphan girls of Jerez in need of a dowry to marry. What remained of de Soto's belongings on the march Moscoso sold at auction—5 slaves, 3 horses, and 700 pigs (200 cruzados each), which the men bought on credit against future profits of gold and silver. According to Elvas, some of the men rejoiced at the change of leadership, believing that Moscoso "who was given to leading a gay life, preferred to see himself at ease in a land of Christians, rather than continue the toils of war."

By consensus, the adventurers set out again on foot,

The death of the adelantado, who perished on the banks of the Mississippi River from the ravages of a fever at the age of 42 on May 21, 1542. One of his officers, Luis Moscoso, succeeded him at the helm of the expedition, much to the relief of many of the men, who were growing weary of de Soto and his merciless, endless journey of destruction.

west to New Spain. They did not trust their seafaring ability without equipment; on the walking route to Mexico they might luck into riches. From June until October, they hiked steadily, crossing the Red River in the neighborhood of Shreveport, Louisiana, and veering southwest into the dry plains of Texas—the Province of the Herdsmen. Moscoso repeated de Soto's practice of extorting grain, porters, and guides, whom the new adelantado tortured, hanged, or cast to the dogs for misleading the invaders. (The Spaniards' lack of a translator contributed to the communication problem.) In the sparsely settled barrens near Daycao—perhaps the Brazos River, which runs south from Waco, Texas—Moscoso finally halted and called a conference. Provisions were extremely low; winter was nearing. Perhaps all that lay ahead was the desert Cabeza de Vaca had described, where nomadic Indians lived on cactus. The captains agreed with their commander that they should return to the Mississippi and try to sail down it into the Gulf of Mexico.

Not all the troops concurred with the decision. In eastern Texas they had seen Indian trade goods from the western Pueblo, such as turquoise and cotton shawls, but those who wanted to pursue this new treasure could not override the motion to retreat. In two months, the Spaniards retraced their steps to Anilco, sorry that they had laid waste to the countryside on the way out. Some of the Indians in Louisiana had rebuilt and replanted—but not at Anilco, where the army's occupation the previous spring had disrupted sowing.

In miserable December winds, the Spanish searched for a province where the autumn harvest had been successful. They found it to the northeast, at Aminoya on the Mississippi above present-day Natchez. Since de Soto's death, the Spaniards had covered more than 780 miles, but the journey had been costly. Many expeditioners and most of the Indian captives died of exposure, hunger, and exhaustion.

In an eerie replay of the Narváez expedition, the remnants of the army began building seven boats with which to brave the river, the gulf, and, if all went well, the Caribbean. Thanks to de Soto's foresight in staffing his venture, however, this group succeeded better than the earlier one. Maestro Franco, the Genoese engineer, supervised the construction, helped by four or five Biscayan carpenters. One of the Portuguese, who had learned the technique as a prisoner of war in Morocco, taught the troops to saw lumber. The Genoese and Sardinian caulkers sealed the planks with oakum pitch. Although he was extremely ill for most of that spring of 1543, the cooper managed to make two half-hogshead water barrels for each ship. The Spaniards melted slave chains into nails, wove cables from mulberry bark, and formed anchors from stirrups. Local Indians contributed ropes, shawls for sails, and so much corn for sustenance that by the end of winter they were begging for relief from starvation.

The work came to a halt in March when heavy spring

Fearing the Indians would find it if buried on land, Moscoso had the adelantado's body buried in the Mississippi River. Here, a 19th-century artist has depicted the river burial as an eerie, moonlit ceremony. The attempt at subterfuge was unnecessary, as the Indians had never believed Moscoso's story that de Soto was away on a visit to his god.

rains caused the Mississippi to breach its natural levees. The Spaniards saved their horses by tethering them to rafts and continued their work as best they could from platforms built on stilts. The flood receded by the beginning of May; a second spell of high water in June enabled the voyagers to float their vessels to the river. On the banks of the Mississippi, the Spanish killed and salted the hogs and about 30 lame horses. The remaining two dozen mounts were strapped two hooves to a canoe and towed behind the ships. On Moscoso's orders, all but the most influential officers abandoned their Indian slaves—about 500 in all— who wept because they had converted to Christianity voluntarily, Elvas said, and now were stranded among foreign tribes. On an evening in early July 1543, the survivors of the expedition—roughly half of the 600 who had landed 4 years earlier—boarded the 7 makeshift brigantines and cast off. On the water, the Spanish did not conduct themselves much differently than they had on land. During the day, the soldiers put to shore to steal grain, as usual. When some Indians objected, the Spanish burned down their town. The next day an armada of canoes—estimated by Elvas to number more than 100, with more than 60 braves in each—tailed the Spanish flotilla. When the Indians made unfriendly overtures, Juan de Guzman and more

As had the Narváez expedition, the de Soto party constructed their own boats to reach the safety of more welcoming environs of New Spain than the American Southwest. As the flotilla descended the Mississippi, the Spaniards were harrassed by Indian tribes seeking revenge for previous mistreatment.

than a dozen of his infantrymen took to the canoes that the ships were towing and paddled into the midst of the enemy. Dodging swords, the Indians surrounded and capsized the canoes. Most of the Spaniards, who were garbed in their heavy armor, sank immediately; the natives clubbed the rest to death with their paddles.

For the next two weeks, Indians hounded the strangers. At first the soldiers hid under their ship's deck, but with no one manning the oars, the vessels had a tendency to swing wildly in the river's strong current. Accordingly, the Spaniards began taking turns shielding the rowers, so the Indians targeted the horses instead. Attempts to protect the horses so slowed the voyage that Moscoso ordered a party to take the animals ashore, slaughter them, and cure the meat. Once on the river's banks, some of the steeds galloped off as if they were aware of their imminent fate; their flight terrified the local Indians.

Finally, near the mouth of the Mississippi, the natives gave up the chase. Fearful of capsizing, the voyagers resisted, accepted, then rejected Juan de Añasco's suggestion of taking a shortcut across the gulf to Mexico. Instead, for most of the next month they hugged the coast, fishing, bickering, and swatting mosquitoes. Although storms tossed and buffeted the small ships and the crews were tortured by thirst, the Spaniards nevertheless arrived intact at the mouth of the Pánuco, where local Indians directed them upriver to the nearby Spanish settlement. "The pleasure that all received at this news cannot be sufficiently expressed," Elvas reported. "Many, leaping on shore, kissed the ground; and all, on bended knees, with hands raised above them, and their eyes to heaven, remained untiring in giving thanks to God."

The 311 survivors—haggard, sunburned, and dressed in skins—caused a stir in Pánuco, where the humble townspeople welcomed them as sons. After a messenger informed the viceroy, Don Antonio de Mendoza, of their arrival, he dispatched clothes, medicine, supplies, even pomegranates from Mexico City, about 150 miles from the coast. Yet as the adventurers began to recover, they contrasted the poverty of Pánuco with the fertility of Florida. Regrets and recriminations festered, and the soldiers who had wanted to continue on overland went on a rampage against the officers who had voted for the sea retreat.

On the orders of the viceroy, in early October the de Soto expeditioners set out on the last leg of their journey—divided into small, more easily subdued groups of 20 or 30 foot soldiers or horsemen. Altogether they had covered 3,000 miles on land (roughly the length of the United States from the Atlantic to the Pacific), 1,100 miles on water. Once in Mexico City, they disbanded. Many returned to Spain; almost as many joined the ongoing conquest and fighting in Peru; some, including Ranjel and Biedma, stayed on in Mexico.

Many historians have dismissed the de Soto expedition as a wasted effort, a testimony to the adventurousness and hardiness of the Spanish certainly, but in many ways little more than an exercise in wanton brutality. Its leader was killed, it inspired no immediate colonization, and it uncovered no new source of wealth. De Soto's claim to fame as discoverer of the Mississippi probably belongs to Pineda, and his most tangible contribution to North America was hogs: The razorback descendants of those that escaped from the Spanish herd fed the pioneers and still populate the thickets of the South.

The ill will he left behind haunted later European contacts with Native Americans. When the peaceable Dominican Fray Luis de Cancer set out to mend relations with the Florida Indians in 1549, he mistakenly dropped anchor in Bahia Espíritu Santo. Despite warnings from Muñoz, the hostage page from de Soto's trip who escaped to the friars' ship, Cancer and at least two other monks went ashore unarmed with a plea for friendship. The natives scalped them. From this point on, missionaries rarely ventured anywhere in Florida without an armed guard, which tended to compromise their message of brotherhood.

De Soto's ruthlessness outraged 16th-century intellectuals as much as it has contemporary scholars. In his *Brief Account of the Destruction of the Indies*, Las Casas condemned the "tyrant-governor" and his "vile deeds" against "a population that was wise, well disposed, politically well organized." The crusading bishop reported that when one of the Indian porters crumbled under his load, de Soto's men lopped off his head at the neck so as not to slow down the march of other slaves on the same chain: "The head fell to one side of the road, while the body fell to the other." Although Gonzalo Fernández de Oviedo, one of the first historians of the New World, did not hold such a high opinion of natives—in his view they were often lazy and vicious—he found in Ranjel's account of de Soto's march much to criticize. The expedition, Oviedo felt, "caused alteration and desolation of the land and loss of liberty of people, without making Christians or friends." To Francisco Lopez de Gomara, who published a history of the Indies in 1554, de Soto failed because he did not establish settlements before he started searching for gold or silver mines.

On land the men of the de Soto expedition were an awesome military force, but on water they were no match for the Indians. Without their horses and guns, the Spaniards were easily defeated by the wily Native Americans. In this engraving, the Indians surround the Spaniards and force them into the water where many, weighted down by armor or simply beaten by the Indians with oars, sank to the sandy bottom.

King Philip II of Spain. When France attempted to establish colonies in Florida and the Caribbean, Philip, the son of Charles I, dispatched veteran captain Pedro Menéndez de Avilés to crush the French and establish Spanish colonies there.

Ironically, given de Soto's murderous lack of respect for the Indians' way of life, modern-day anthropologists value accounts of the expedition for their descriptions of indigenous culture and wildlife. In recounting the capture of Diego Muñoz, for instance, the Inca sets this scene: The Spaniards trespassed into the "great enclosures of dry rock" the Indians had built to trap skates and other fish washed in by high tide; when the water receded, the harvest was already drying in the sun. The Gentleman of Elvas often paused in his narrative to observe how the Indians dressed or what they ate. He devoted half a page to the fish of Arkansas—the one the Indians called *pereo* with rows of teeth, another with the head of a familiar hake but colored red and brown. Similarly, Elvas carefully recorded his observations of salt making in Arkansas:

> As they cannot gather the salt without a large mixture of sand, it is thrown together into certain baskets they have for their purpose, made large at the mouth and small at the bottom. These are set in the air on a ridge-pole; and water being thrown on, vessels are placed under them wherein it may fall; then, being strained and placed on the fire, it is boiled away, leaving salt at the bottom.

De Soto's exploration therefore afforded a rare glimpse of native culture before it was permanently altered by prolonged trade and contact with Europeans.

Finally, de Soto's fiasco did shape the future of Florida—not as a gold mine but as a shipping base. In the 1540s, the Spaniards discovered mammoth silver deposits in Zacatecas and Guanajuato in north central Mexico. This precious metal was shipped back to Spain from the gulf port of Veracruz. Passing through the Straits of Florida on the way to Spain, however, the treasure fleet was exposed to three hazards: the channel, with its shallow water and coral reefs; the weather, particularly hurricanes; and French privateers. A settlement on the peninsula would provide a harbor where ships could wait out storms and local seamen could salvage shipwrecked crews and cargo and defend against pirates.

Luis de Velasco, viceroy of New Spain, envisioned two Florida colonies—one on the east coast, in the islands off South Carolina, and one on the gulf coast. A road across the peninsula, on which the Spaniards could portage heavy or valuable cargo as the vessels navigated around the cape, would connect the two.

In 1559, Tristán de Luna y Arellano, son of the governor of the Yucatán in Mexico, set out to establish the gulf port at Achusi, as de Soto's captain Maldonado had christened present-day Pensacola Bay. Fifteen hundred pioneers enlisted with de Luna, including Biedma, Ranjel, and several other veterans of the de Soto expedition, but a hurricane destroyed most of their supplies as they unloaded at Achusi. That fall, a large contingent of the would-be colonists hiked into Alabama. Although the Indians shared their stores, by spring the soldiers were reduced to eating ground acorns, which the women and children found so bitter that they foraged for leaves and twigs instead. After the adventurous men and women spent another year roaming and mooching off the natives, the venture folded.

The French, meanwhile, were preparing to stake claims on the East Coast. Despite Spain's attempt at secrecy—to keep buzzing flies away from its morsels, as historian Woodbury Lowery put it—spies and informants had infiltrated the cosmopolitan ports of Seville and Cádiz. French pirates frequently pillaged Havana and preyed upon ships carrying sugar, hides, and cassia (a medicinal herb). (Spanish ships carrying more valuable cargo tended to be better protected.) The Spanish also worried that the French might foment a revolt among the black Africans whom the Spanish were importing in large numbers to toil on the plantations of the West Indies, the Indians there being by now all but extinct.

In 1562, the Frenchmen Jean Ribault and René Goulaine de Laudonnière carried out a seaborne reconnaissance off the coast from Florida's Cape Canaveral to the sea islands off Georgia. Two years later, Laudonnière and about 300 pioneers alighted south of present-day Jacksonville on the St. Johns River, where, amid cedars, palms, and laurels, they built Fort Caroline on a high bluff. But the French, like the Spanish, antagonized the local Indians, preferring to extort food from the residents rather than plant their own crops. Discontent soon grew epidemic; malcontents threatened mutiny, and one group made the mistake of raiding Spanish Jamaica. When King Philip II, son and successor of Charles I, learned of France's effrontery—and of its plans to send more soldiers, families, and craftsmen to Fort Caroline with Ribault—he deputized the distinguished sea dog Pedro Menéndez de Avilés to root out the French colony and plant a Spanish one.

Menéndez's arrival in Florida in September 1565 coincided with Ribault's, but weather favored the Spaniards. Menéndez docked his fleet at an inlet about 40 miles south of Fort Caroline. Rallying the settlers to his decks, Ribault decided to strike by sea, but a fierce storm shipwrecked his fleet. Menéndez faced almost no opposition when he marched into the French fort. Women and children were imprisoned and deported, but when Menéndez captured the stranded sailors, he executed all but a few Catholics, musicians, and stragglers.

Menéndez went on to found St. Augustine, today the oldest city in North America. As the governor of Florida, he was frequently called away on royal business that took him all over the peninsula and up the East Coast, but he nonetheless engaged in successful negotiations with the Indians, sponsored Jesuit missions, and searched in vain for a sea passage to China. The territory de Soto had wandered over aimlessly, Menéndez succeeded in colonizing and administering.

Although Florida changed hands several times before becoming the 27th of the United States in 1845, its Spanish legacy has contributed to its modern cosmopolitanism. De Soto's blood-drenched trek, like other journeys of exploration, was one of the wedges that was instrumental in opening the North American continent to European colonization. Reflecting its Spanish heritage, Florida remains linked, both culturally and politically, to the Caribbean and Latin America, but subsequent pioneers were more likely to have been lured by the availability of land or vistas of sunshine reflecting off the placid waters by a sandy beach than the prospect of finding gold nuggets in a rushing stream.

Pedro Menéndez de Avilés, whose forces met little resistance from the French when they arrived in Florida in September 1565. Menéndez went on to found the oldest city in North America, St. Augustine, and finally succeeded in establishing a permanent Spanish presence on the Florida peninsula.

Further Reading

Biedma, Luis Hernandez de, and Elvas. *Narratives of the Career of Hernando de Soto.* Translated by Buckingham Smith. Gainesville, FL: Palmetto Books, 1968.

Blacker, Irwin R., and Harry M. Rosen. *The Golden Conquistadores.* Indianapolis: Bobbs-Merrill, 1960.

Deforneaux, Marcelin. *Daily Life in Spain in the Golden Age.* Stanford: Stanford University Press, 1970.

Dibble, Ernest F., and Earle W. Newton, eds. *Spain and Her Rivals on the Gulf Coast.* Pensacola, FL: Historic Pensacola Preservation Board, 1971.

Garcilaso de la Vega. *The Florida of the Inca.* Edited and translated by John G. Varner and Jeanette J. Varner. Austin: University of Texas Press, 1962.

Grant, Matthew. *De Soto: Explorer of the Southeast.* Mankato, MN: Creative Education, 1974.

Hemming, John. *The Conquest of the Incas.* New York: Harcourt Brace Jovanovich, 1970.

Las Casas, Bartolomé de. *The Devastation of the Indies: A Brief Account.* Translated by Herma Briffault. New York: The Seabury Press, 1974.

Lloyd, Alan. *The Spanish Centuries.* Garden City, NY: Doubleday, 1968.

Lyon, Eugene. *The Enterprise of Florida: Pedro Menendez de Aviles and the Spanish Conquest of 1565–1568.* Gainesville: The University Presses of Florida, 1976.

McKendrick, Melveena. *Ferdinand and Isabella.* New York: American Heritage, 1968.

Pennington, Piers. *The Great Explorers: Stories of Men Who Discovered and Mapped Unknown Areas of the World.* New York: Facts on File, 1979.

Morison, Samuel Eliot. *The European Discovery of America: The Southern Voyages, 1492–1616.* New York: Oxford University Press, 1974.

Sanderlin, George, ed. *Bartolemé de Las Casas: A Selection of His Writings.* New York: Knopf, 1971.

Schell, Rolfe F. *De Soto Didn't Land at Tampa.* Ft. Myers Beach, FL: Island Press, 1966.

Tourtellot, Jonathan B., ed. *Into the Unknown: The Story of Exploration.* Washington, DC: National Geographic Society, 1987.

Weddle, Robert S. *Spanish Sea: The Gulf of Mexico in North American Discovery, 1500–1685.* College Station: Texas A&M University Press, 1985.

Chronology

Entries in roman type refer directly to de Soto and the exploration of the American South; entries in italics refer to important historical and cultural events of the era.

ca. 1474   Juan Ponce de León born

1492   Christopher Columbus reaches the Caribbean island of Hispaniola by sailing west in his search of a passage to China

1493   Ponce de León signs on to Columbus's second voyage to the New World

1497   *Portuguese sailor Vasco da Gama rounds the Cape of Good Hope, opening a sea route to India*

1500   Hernando de Soto born in Jerez de los Cabelleros, Spain

1508–10   Ponce de León conquers Puerto Rico

1512   *Italian painter Michelangelo completes Sistine Chapel ceiling frescoes*

1513   Ponce de Léon lands on the east coast of Florida somewhere between present-day Daytona and New Smyrna Beach; *Vasco Nuñez de Balboa discovers the Pacific Ocean*

1517   *Martin Luther posts his Ninety-five Theses on the door of Schlosskirche in Wittenberg; German Reformation begins*

1518   *Portuguese navigator Ferdinand Magellan embarks on his journey to circumnavigate the globe*

1521   Ponce de León dies of an arrow wound in Havana

1523   De Soto serves as an officer under Francisco Fernández de Córdoba on a mission to oust a rival of Pedro Arias Dávila's in Nicaragua; Córdoba decides to take the colony for himself; de Soto opposes this act of treason and is thrown in jail

1530–32   Signs on as an officer with Francisco Pizarro and proceeds to plunder the Inca cities in Peru

1534	*First voyage of French explorer Jacques Cartier to North America*
1533–36	De Soto serves as a lieutenant governor for Pizarro in Cuzco; returns to Spain in 1536 to hero's welcome
1537	Receives permission from the Crown to explore, colonize, and look for gold in Florida
1539	Reaches the western coast of Florida with a crew of about 600 and claims it as a possession of Spain's in the name of King Charles I
1540	Meets La Señora of Cofitachequi, a Creek princess, who bestows pearls and gold on him; takes her prisoner; he and his men become the first Europeans to cross the Appalachians
May 1541	Reaches the banks of the Mississippi River
May 1542	Dies of a fever, probably malaria or typhoid
1542–43	Last remnants of the de Soto expedition reach Mexico City

Index

Achusi, 76, 103
Ais, 92
Alabama River, 83
Alaminos, Anton de, 30, 34, 35–36, 37
Añasco, Juan de, 67, 69, 70, 75, 76, 88, 93, 99
Añasco Bay, 26, 27
Ancilla River, 75
Andes Mountains, 50, 53
Apalache, 24, 40, 42, 74, 75, 76
Appalachian Mountains, 81
Arias Dávila, Pedro, 47, 48, 55
Arias, Gomez, 76
Arkansas River, 91
Asinai, 92
Atahuallpa, 51–53
Aute, 42
Aztecs, 20, 49–50, 54

Bahía de Caballos (Bay of Horses), 43
Balboa, Vasco Núñez de, 47, 50
Bermudez, Diego, 30
Biedma, Luis Hernandez de, 15, 16, 90, 100, 103
Bimini, 28, 29, 34
Bobadilla, Isabel de, 55
Bobadilla, Leonor de, 66, 67
Brief Account of the Destruction of the Indies, A (Las Casas), 101
Buono de Quexo, Juan, 30
Burns Island, 81

Cabeza de Vaca, Alvar Núñez, 38, 40, 42, 44–45, 65, 96
Cabo de las Corrientos (Cape of the Currents), 32
Caddo, 91
Cádiz, 26, 103

Cajamarca, 51, 52, 53
Calderon, Pedro, 72, 75–76
Caliquen, 74
Calusa, 32
Campeche, Bay of, 49
Canary Islands, 66
Cancer, Fray Luis de, 100
Capacheguy River, 77
Cardenosa, Alonso Romo de, 66
Carib, 34
Castellamos, Juan de, 35
Castile, Spain, 29, 38
Castillo, 45
Ceron, Juan, 28
Charles I, king of Spain, 14, 36, 38, 56, 69, 93
Cherokee, 81
Chiaha, 81, 82
Chickasaw, 87–88
Chicora, 36
Choctaw, 43
Cofitachequi, 78–79
Colorado River, 45
Columbus, Christopher, 26, 27, 29, 30, 36
Columbus, Diego, 28
Companon, Francisco, 48
Coosa River, 79
Copoque, 44
Córdoba, Francisco Fernández de, 47–48
Córdoba, Hernandez de, 35, 36
Cortés, Hernán, 49, 50, 51
Council of the Indies, 38, 66
Creek, 77, 79, 83
Cuba, 35, 40, 56, 66, 67, 76, 86, 93
Cuzco, 53, 54

De Almagro, Diego, 50, 54
De Luna y Arellano, Tristán, 103
De Soto, Diego, 22
De Soto, Hernando
  appointed governor of Cuba, 56
  conquest of Incas and, 47–55

death, 93
discovers Mississippi, 89–90
fights battle at Napituca, 13–17, 20–23
in Florida, 13–17, 20–23, 69–77
historical legacy, 100–103
marries Isabel de Bobadilla, 55
roams American South, 77–79, 81–89
Dias de Aux, Miguel, 28
Dorantos, Andres, 45
Dry Tortugas, 33

Ecuador, 50, 56
Elvas, Gentleman of, 15, 22, 55, 65, 70, 73, 74–75, 77, 78, 79, 81, 85, 90, 92, 93, 95, 98, 99, 102
Espindola, Cristobal de, 65
Estevanico, 45

Ferdinand, king of Spain, 25, 27, 28
Florida, 13, 14, 17, 21, 31–32, 34, 35, 36, 37, 38, 40, 42, 56, 65, 67, 69, 73, 74, 76, 77, 79, 86, 100, 102–3, 104, 105
Fort Caroline, 104
Franco, Maestro, 97

Gallegos, Baltasor de, 65, 70, 84, 88
Garay, Francisco de, 37
Garcia, Diego, 66
Garcilaso de la Vega, 15–16, 21, 70–71, 76, 77, 78, 91, 102
Gaytan, Juan, 86
Gomara, Francisco Lopez de, 101
Granada, Spain, 25
Guachoya, 92–93
Guayaquil, Gulf of, 50
Gulf of California, 45

Gulf of Mexico, 21, 37, 51,
   96, 102
Guzman, Juan de, 92, 98

Han, 44
Havana, Cuba, 35, 36, 38,
   67, 76, 79, 103
Herrera y Tordesillas,
   Antonio de, 28, 29
Higüey Province, 27
Hinestrosa, Francisca de, 88
Hirrihigua, 40–41, 70, 71
Hispaniola, 26, 27, 28, 36
Hiwassee River, 81

Iberian Peninsula, 25
Incas, 14, 20, 50, 51,
   52–53, 54
Isabella, queen of Spain,
   25, 27, 29

Jerez de los Caballeros,
   Spain, 47
Jiminez, Beatriz, 29
Jiminez, Jana, 29

Las Casas, Bartolomé de,
   35, 101
La Señora de Cofitachequi,
   78–79, 81
Laudonnière, René
   Goulaine de, 104
Los Martires, (the Martyrs),
   32

Maldonado, Francisco, 76,
   79, 86, 103
Marquesas Keys, 32
Martin, Alonso, 66
Mauvilla, 83–86, 88, 91
Mendoza, Don Antonio de,
   99
Menéndez de Avilés, Pedro,
   104
Mexico, 14, 20, 37, 38, 43,
   49, 54, 72, 96, 102
Mexico City, 50, 100
Miruelo, Diego, 35, 40
Mississippi River, 37, 44, 88,
   92, 95, 96, 98, 99, 100

Mobile Bay, 44
Mocozo, 72, 75, 76
Morison, Samuel Eliot, 38
Moscoso de Alvarado, Luis,
   55, 66, 70, 73, 83, 87,
   88, 93, 95, 96, 98, 99
Muñoz, Diego, 76, 100,
   102

Napituca, 13, 15, 16, 17,
   21, 75, 76
Narváez, Pánfilo de, 25,
   37–44, 45, 56, 70, 74,
   75, 89, 97
Nicaragua, 47, 48
Nuñez de Guzmán, Pedro,
   25
Nuño de, Tobar, 55, 66,
   67, 85, 92

Orinoco River, 29
Ortega, Francisco de, 29
Ortiz, Juan, 13, 17, 70–71,
   78, 87, 92
Ortubia, Juan Perez de, 30,
   34
Ouachita River, 92
Ovando, Nicolás de, 27
Oviedo, Gonzalo Fernández
   de, 101

Panama, 47, 48
Pánuco, 99–100
Paracoxi, 23, 72
Pecos River, 45
Perico, 76, 78
Peru, 14, 20, 38, 50, 54,
   55, 72, 100
Philip II, king of Spain, 104
Pineda, Alvarez de, 37, 89,
   100
Piura Valley, 50
Pizarro, Francisco, 14, 50,
   51, 52–53, 54
Ponce, Hernan, 95
Ponce de León, Juan, 25,
   27–29, 30–35, 36, 47
Porcallo de Figueroa,
   Vasco, 67, 70, 72
Pueblo, 96
Puerto Rico, 26, 27, 34

Ranjel, Rodrigo, 15, 78,
   81, 85, 87, 90, 91, 100,
   101
Ribault, Jean, 104
Rio de Las Palmas, 38
Rodriguez Lobillo, Juan, 55

St. Augustine, 104
St. Johns River, 104
Saldana, Francisco de,
   22–23
Sanibel Island, 34
San Salvador, 30
Savannah River, 78
Sechura Desert, 50
Seville, Spain, 55, 65, 103
Sierra Madre, 45
Sonora River, 45
Spain, 25–26, 29, 34, 45,
   49, 50, 53, 73, 100
Suwannee River, 41, 75

Taino, 27
Tampa Bay, 40
Tascaluza, 83
Tennessee River, 81
Tenochtitlán, 49
Teodoro, Doroteo, 43, 44
Texas, 44, 96
Timicua, 38, 41
Tinoco, Arias, 66
Tobar, Nuño de, 55, 66,
   67, 85, 92
Trinidad, 38
Tumbes, 50

Vasconcelos, Andre de, 65,
   66
Vazquez de Ayllón, Lucas,
   36–37, 56, 79
Velasco, Luis de, 103
Veracruz, Mexico, 49
Vitachuco, 13–14, 16, 17,
   21–22, 23

Withlacoochee River, 41

Yucatán Peninsula, 35

Zacatecas, 102

Picture Credits

Sylvia Whitman holds a B.A. in folklore and mythology from Harvard University as well as an M.A. in American studies from the University of Texas at Austin. She resides in Orlando, Florida, and has written many articles on history and exploration.

William H. Goetzmann holds the Jack S. Blanton, Sr., Chair in History at the University of Texas at Austin, where he has taught for many years. The author of numerous works on American history and exploration, he won the 1967 Pulitzer and Parkman prizes for his *Exploration and Empire: The Role of the Explorer and Scientist in the Winning of the American West, 1800–1900*. With his son William N. Goetzmann, he coauthored *The West of the Imagination*, which received the Carr P. Collins Award in 1986 from the Texas Institute of Letters. His documentary television series of the same name received a blue ribbon in the history category at the American Film and Video Festival held in New York City in 1987. A recent work, *New Lands, New Men: America and the Second Great Age of Discovery*, was published in 1986 to much critical acclaim.

Michael Collins served as command module pilot on the *Apollo 11* space mission, which landed his colleagues Neil Armstrong and Buzz Aldrin on the moon. A graduate of the United States Military Academy, Collins was named an astronaut in 1963. In 1966 he piloted the *Gemini 10* mission, during which he became the third American to walk in space. The author of several books on space exploration, Collins was director of the Smithsonian Institution's National Air and Space Museum from 1971 to 1978 and is a recipient of the Presidential Medal of Freedom.